Lines on Lebanon

Palewell Press

Lines on Lebanon

Antony Johae

Lines on Lebanon
First edition 2025 from Palewell Press, www.palewellpress.co.uk
Printed and bound in the UK

ISBN 978-1-911587-89-7

All Rights Reserved. Copyright © 2025 Antony Johae. No part of this publication may be reproduced or transmitted in any form or by any means, without permission in writing from the author. The right of Antony Johae to be identified as the author of this work has been asserted by him in accordance with the Copyright, Designs and Patents Act 1988

The cover design is Copyright © 2025 Camilla Reeve
The front cover photo of the view over the Roman ruins of the Temple of Bacchus, the little temple, in Byblos, Lebanon, was purchased and downloaded from iStock photo ID:621136004
The photo of Antony Johae next to his biography is Copyright © 2025 Antony Johae

A CIP catalogue record for this title is available from the British Library.

Acknowledgements

Thanks to the editors of the following publications where versions have previously appeared: "Search after Hitchcock" in *The Frogmore Papers* 81 (Spring 2013); "Service" in *Blast Furnace* 5.3 (December 21, 2015); "Going West and East" in *Panorama: The Journal of Intelligent Travel* (War and Peace issue, 2019); and "Permit, Passport, Parking" in *The Frogmore Papers* 96 (Autumn 2020).

For those who lost their lives in the Beirut Port explosion, 4th August, 2020

Contents

Introduction 1
Part One: Lines on Landing 3
    Going West and East 4
    Greeting 12
Part Two: Lines on Living 13
    Service 14
    Search after Hitchcock 16
    Washing Ill-Temper Away 18
    Permit, Passport, Parking 19
    Down South 21
    Bekaa's Bounty 25
    Cold Fruit 26
    Christmas Nuggets 29
    A Maid Looks into a Mirror 31
    Slow Coach 32
    Teta Marie's Walk 34
    Three Sisters 37
    Among the Classics 40
    Book Sale at Jbail 41
Part Three: Border Lines 45
    Storm 46
    In a Mountain Village 48
    Shoes 50
    Exchanges 51
    On the Eco-Road 52
    Salon Smells 54
    Water and Waste 57
    La débâcle se poursuit 59
    The Reservoir 60
    Generator Joke 62

Petrol Stationary 64
The Camp 65
Dilemma of a Bank Clerk 67
On the Road to Tripoli 70
On a Tripoli Street 71
At a Beirut Pharmacy 73
Safe 75
At a Bank in Beirut 77
On the Hour – More or Less 83
A Commemoration 84
War Returns 86

Part Four: Last Lines 89

Lebanon: An Unlikely Utopia 90

Antony Johae - Biography 97

Introduction

These are lines on Lebanon – lines written about Lebanon, lines of approach to Lebanon, and lines of communication, which frequently get snarled up and become a tangle at both political and every-day practical levels.

Lebanon is a small mountainous country, bordering on the Mediterranean Sea, with a population of 5.2 million – approximately seventy per cent Moslem and thirty per cent Christian. In addition, and largely as a result of the decade-long civil war in Syria, there are nearly two million refugees living in Lebanon, not including nearly half a million Palestinians who reside in twelve official refugee camps. Clearly, the country is burdened beyond belief. Small wonder the occurrence of frequent crises: daily power cuts, sporadic demonstrations, failures of government, economic collapse and consequent impoverishment.

Events in the book begin during the Lebanese Civil War but quickly move into peaceful times. My first visit was in 1985 when Thérèse and I were married. The early account, "Going West and East", is partly based on that occasion during the conflict, when hostage-taking was making headline news. In 2009, nearly twenty years after the fighting had stopped, we retired and moved to Lebanon, although visits to Thérèse's family had been frequent in the intervening years.

In my *Lines on Lebanon,* I have endeavoured to render an insightful view of life in this vibrant culture as it is lived out from one day to the next, emerging as it has from civil strife and, latterly, its plunge into economic and political crisis. But these are, for the most part, personal impressions borne out of experience living within the society. Sometimes imagination has played a part in embellishing narrative, as in a work of fiction, so that facts become coloured in the creative process. These "impressions", written in colour, range from a domestic family day to a public ceremony commemorating Lebanon's military heroes; from negotiating state bureaucracy to coping with water shortage; from a visit to a Palestinian refugee camp to contact with a Syrian worker; and from enduring constant power cuts to witnessing economic collapse.

These "impressions" (written responses in prose) are at times satirical, at others praiseworthy; at times humorous, at others sombre in tone; at times lyrical, at others, mundane. I hope they will appeal to non-Arab readers, to the huge Lebanese diaspora dispersed around the globe, to the many speakers of English in the Arab world and to the Lebanese population who live and seek to survive in their homeland.

My thanks are due to my wife, Thérèse, to my daughter, Christina, and my son-in-law, Nazih, who have shared this personal journey with me; to members of the Colchester Scribbles Writing Group for critiquing a majority of the text, and to my publisher, Camilla Reeve at Palewell Press, for her editorial guidance.

Antony Johae

Part One: Lines on Landing

1985/1991

Going West and East

It was in 1985 that Thérèse and I met and were married at the registry office in Colchester, my home town. Thérèse had gone ahead to Lebanon to inform her family and to prepare for a church ceremony.

In Beirut, the fighting between factions had resumed after the Israeli army had withdrawn from the city. The Green Line, or the *khutut at tammas* as the Beirutis called it, the no-man's land which divided Muslim West Beirut from the Christian East, could not be crossed by Europeans like myself, and even local men traversed the space from one side to the other at their peril.

I did meet a Muslim in East Beirut, a supplier of spare parts for cars, who seemed to be on the best of terms with his Christian counterpart.

"You think I hate him?" he questioned me, placing his arm around the other man's shoulder.

"It doesn't look like it," I said.

"You think this is a war between Christians and Muslims?" he quizzed me again.

"That is certainly what the world has been led to believe," I replied, although I knew that others on the outside were implicated. I felt uncomfortable as the two men clung to each other and fixed me with their stares. They were not going to allow me to remain an innocent bystander, and at that moment I saw myself more separated from them than they had ever been from one another.

I was not always made to feel like an interloper, and once the civil war was over and I was living in Lebanon with Thérèse and our daughter, Christina, the sight of European construction companies demolishing the ruins of the old Beirut and beginning the reconstruction of the new business centre, made me feel a certain proud involvement in the city's rejuvenation. Beirut might again establish itself as a paragon of the business world, and Lebanon might once more become a trading nation as it had been before the civil war and, too, many centuries earlier when supplying King Solomon with cedars for Elohim's temple; or as when the ancient Phoenicians had traded purple cloth from Tyre, crafted fine furniture from mountain timber, and fashioned jewellery from precious stones, renowned among the veiled women of Arabia.

I recall how it had seemed to me impossible that this country had once prospered in peace. The airport to the south of Beirut had been closed for some time, and even had there been no shelling and the runway had been open, I could not have flown in there, for it was the time of hostage taking. I had landed instead at Damascus. Thérèse was waiting for me as I exited customs with my luggage. Beside her stood a tall man who stepped forward to take one of my bags.

"This is Youssef," Thérèse said. "He has come to take us back to Lebanon."

As we shook hands, he spoke: "You come from London. There are many beautiful buildings, yes?"

I nodded.

"But in Lebanon buildings are knocked down by fire."

"One day they will be built again."

Youssef smiled at my response and led us to his taxi.

Even before we had set off from the Syrian capital, I felt nervous; there was a heavy strangeness about the place which I had not experienced in other foreign cities – ominous almost, and tangible. Perhaps it was the many soldiers milling about the streets, or loaded onto trucks giving the impression of readiness for war; or the accident encountered on the way from the airport – a lorry skewed across the road and the sparkling of an acetylene burner as a crowd surrounded a squashed car trying to get the passengers out; or was it simply that I would soon be inside Lebanon and that I was projecting my fears onto this, the oldest of inhabited cities? I was certainly not entering triumphantly as the Macedonian general had done when driving out the Assyrians, nor like Lawrence when routing the Turks. I felt more like Saul of Tarsus humbled on the Straight Road as he travelled towards Damascus.

Before heading for the border and the Bekaa Valley, Youssef had stopped for us to buy cakes, which Thérèse informed me were cheaper in the Syrian capital than in Beirut. There was no air-conditioning in the car, the afternoon sun was hot, and the back of my damp shirt clung to the seat. I was made thirsty by the sweet cake Youssef offered – *baklawa* he said it was called – and which he would not allow me to refuse.

Once past the frontier, we stopped at a roadside café, but the drink I had chosen was as sweet to the tongue as the cakes had been – a green syrup diluted with water which had, from the look of it, promised the freshness of mint. As we sat in front of the café, two grotesque tanks ground by, followed by several truckloads of soldiers.

"Syrians," Youssef said confidingly. "We will be stopped in the mountains. You know that they are here, don't you?" I did know, but the reality of it struck me as bizarre – a foreign force come, not to invade, but to keep local factions from each other's throats.

The sun descended behind the range as we left the last town in the Bekaa valley before the ascent to the pass.

"The Druze live here," Thérèse explained as we entered a mountain village. "Once Christians lived here too, but they were driven out."

It was dark by now and I could see nobody in the street. Some of the houses looked derelict, while others were boarded up.

"There will be a checkpoint," Youssef said, slowing down. "Syrians – and later Christian militia and the Lebanese army."

A soldier shone his torch into the car. I could not see his face beyond the glare, but his voice sounded friendly. Youssef got out to open up the back for the soldier to look inside. The night air was cool and I shivered in my damp shirt.

Once over the pass we descended, driving through quiet villages until we reached a hill overlooking Beirut. The city lay below, stretching towards a promontory in the west with the sea lying beyond. The water glittered under the moonlight – and then I saw an accompanying flash as though a massive photograph had just been taken; Thérèse pointed out that a shell must have exploded somewhere in the heart of the city, though there was no sound of a detonation. I could vaguely discern a puff of smoke hanging in the air, and at that moment I thought of the city as a diseased body divided against itself.

It was not long before we reached the mountain village of Kornet Chehwan, where Thérèse's mother and father, and her two sisters and two brothers, had been waiting to greet us. In the next week I was introduced to others in the extended family – uncles, aunts, nephews and nieces, cousins and other relatives. I was already beginning to feel thoroughly absorbed into the circle of their lives.

A few days after my arrival, Thérèse and I saw stark evidence of the war in the capital: buildings pockmarked all over by shells, tall office blocks with their windows shattered, gutted houses mere skeletons now, and heaps of rubble of what had once been a mosque, a church, a school, a museum, or a ministry. The centre of the city, where the so-called Green Line passed through, was entirely mutilated and the famed beauty of Beirut gone. The old sandstone buildings, which I had seen in photographs, were shattered, their columns and arrowed windows destroyed.

Although we heard no firing that day, the two-fold bang of Israeli fighter planes flying overhead breaking the sound barrier reminded us of war and the vulnerability of civilians walking or riding in the streets. Our taxi-driver, whose crucifix suspended from his rear-view mirror on a string of worry beads swung with the swerving of the car, crossed himself at every crossroad that we passed; he had reason to because I noticed that there was not a single traffic-light that was working.

That evening, we had been dining at a restaurant in Ashrafieh, a district in East Beirut not far from the port, when the shelling began. Most of the customers and the staff made a quick escape while a few others, unwilling to take the risk, remained. Thérèse and I were too far away from Kornet Chehwan to leave, so when the proprietor ordered us into the basement, we obeyed – and there we stayed for three whole days while the bombardment continued. There were six of us at first: the restaurant proprietor whose name was George, a family of three who lived in the area, and we two, soon to be church married.

It wasn't long before the light from the dangling bulb went out.

"Don't worry," George said in the dark, "the electricity is closed – it is normal." Then I heard a match being struck and, in a few seconds, we could see one another in the intimate light of a candle.

"Don't worry," George said again smiling across at me. "There is my generator. I can open it when it is quiet – and you can lie down there until it is finished." – and he pointed to a pile of blankets and mattresses in a corner of the basement; but at that moment we heard the scream of a missile.

"Under the tables!" George yelled as the room shook in the deafening explosion; there was a strong smell of cordite and the candle went out. I could hear a woman moaning in the dark and the voice of a man speaking in Arabic, then in English, apparently addressing me: "My wife has had enough. It was better when the Israelis were here; at least we knew who was firing at us."

"Now, we don't know," the woman joined in, "and that makes me angry and desperate. What have we done to them, whoever they are, that they should make us suffer? For too long!" – and I could hear her weeping again, and another woman's voice speaking soothingly in Arabic.

Later, with a lull in the bombardment, George left us to start up the generator and, when the bulb lit up, the first thing I saw was a cockroach, its antennae waving, stationary on the floor, seeming to be nonplussed by the sudden light. The woman who had been weeping shuddered and made a move to kill it.

"Leave it," the husband said impatiently, "isn't there room for all of us here?" – with which the cockroach, having adjusted to the light, scuttled out of sight.

"*Araq!*" George announced as he came back into the room with a bottle in one hand and glasses between his fingers in the other.

"The cockroach isn't staying," I said.

"Is that your English humour?" Thérèse asked teasingly – and the others laughed.

If the cockroach shunned our company that night, the mosquitoes didn't. We lay down on the mattresses, but none of us could sleep because of a double assault – the intermittent bombardment outside and the constant zooming in of the long-legged creatures that seemed to have taken possession of the room – so we talked instead.

We learned that the husband had been teaching biochemistry at the American University, but was now made redundant because it was unsafe for Christian men to cross the Green Line to the campus in the west. His wife kept on shaking her head as her husband recounted how he had abandoned his post, and I saw tears in her eyes.

"At first, when the fighting started, I could get across town; there were road blocks of course – militia and armed Palestinians – but it got too dangerous – snipers, weapons everywhere. I haven't been to West Beirut for years."

"He stays at home with me," his wife said. "How long it will go on ... we don't know," and turning to her daughter – "but Nadia's office is on this side, so she can go to work when there's no shelling."

"It's not far from here," Nadia explained. "A solicitor's practice, but since the law courts are hardly functioning, I feel myself unemployed like my father here."

At that moment there was a sudden explosion, perhaps a street or two away, and Nadia jumped up nervously and exchanged words in Arabic with her father.

"What is it?" I asked.

"Nothing," Nadia said, "just a door." She saw me looking puzzled and laughed.

"That's what we say when there's an explosion – just to reassure each other: *La, haitha bab* – No, that's a door."

"Even if the building above you is collapsing?"

"Perhaps not, then it's not just a door."

When finally emerging from our hiding place, I expected to see the restaurant in a state of collapse, but this was not in fact the case; to be sure, every window had been shattered and most of the crockery smashed in the persistent blasts, but the building itself remained intact. With what I was to discover was typical of Lebanese enterprise, George set about having the window glass replaced – for the fifth time since the war had started, so he told me; and two days after the bombardment had stopped, we heard that the restaurant was back in business.

Thérèse and I got to know the Sassin family well during those three days underground; they talked much about what they, and others, had endured in the last ten years; and after we had emerged from the basement, they invited us to dinner at their home. We, in our turn, asked them to our wedding. The ceremony took place in the Greek Orthodox church at Antelias, a town not far along the coast from Beirut, where Thérèse and her family had lived before moving to Kornet Chehwan on Mount Lebanon.

A few days after the wedding, Thérèse and I set out with Youssef, our driver, for the airport at Damascus and took the flight for London.

We did not return to Lebanon until the Spring of 1991, by which time the civil war had ended. Thérèse had been in her teens when the war began and had no recollection of visiting West Beirut except on a shopping expedition with her mother and father to the district of Hamra. Now that it was safe to go, she wanted to see the other side of the city for herself.

It was strange that we should both be visiting this part of Beirut almost for the first time – she, someone who had lived in Antelias, and then Kornet Chehwan, for so many years before her marriage, and I, a tourist so to speak. As we looked out of the window of the bus, we were struck by the devastation; the buildings still standing had been heavily scarred by shells and shrapnel, while those which had been gutted had taken on the shape of a ghost city.

"Was this part of the Green Line?" I asked.

"Yes," Thérèse replied, "and it *is* green, look!" – and it was so, for growing up among the rubble and the ruins you could see grass and weeds and even little trees.

On our way back, we saw a group of young people get on the bus. I noticed that they said little to each other and looked strangely diffident.

"They're going for the first time," Thérèse said. "They've never been before – to the east, just like you and I to the west" – and as we smiled at them, they beamed back shyly.

1985

Greeting

I was new to the Arab world, unfamiliar with its customs, its language almost completely opaque; so that when I arrived in Lebanon to marry my bride, I found myself hiding behind her, linguistically speaking, she being my surrogate voice – my interpreter.

We were to meet the officiating priest in Antelias, but she had left me on a street corner to wait for him, while she popped into a shop to buy cake decoration.

I saw what looked like the priest get out of a car; he was dressed in black and wore a fierce-looking beard. Appearing to recognize me – a European – as the bridegroom-to-be, he crossed the road. As he did so, my brain searched for the Arabic words for "good morning" or "hello" or "How do you do?"

The priest stood sternly in front of me; his eyes pierced me – like Rasputin. Confused, I took his hand to shake it and said, as confidently as I could, "*Mabrouk*", not realizing that it meant "Congratulations".

Part Two: Lines on Living

2009

Service

At Antelias in the late evening we arrive with our shopping on the slope where the taxis wait. He hails us – my wife and I – eager for passengers, perhaps his last run. We tell him "Ain Aar" and he hustles us in with a big woman in the back. The front passenger seat is left unoccupied.

The taxi, back-heavy, snorts up the mountain-side as though in need of a service. A minute – and it stops dead; a work-worn African gets in. The driver seems to know him; he stretches out his hand to ruffle his crinkly hair. Music is on loud – African it sounds or Marley-like. It brings back Ghana, but their talking is Arabic.

Another sudden stop – the African gets out and makes a dash for the shop they call the Wooden Bakery. Taxi still stationary, the driver apologizes to us in the rear. It seems he is waiting for him – an extra service?

Five minutes, and his passenger comes with a bulging bag – gets back in, takes out a roll, and eats. I think: perhaps he's done a long day's work; this is his first food, and the driver pities him.

Setting off again, the taxi zig-zags across the road to the other side weaving in-and-out of head-on cars. I grip the leather seat. "He's going down the mountain!" Thérèse remonstrates. "Sorry, sorry" says the driver turning to the three of us in the back – "Sorry."

We stop – this time for a young man – as though for rendezvous. He squeezes in at the front. The door is squashed shut and – *hamdullah*[1] – the taxi heads up again to Rabieh. We hit hairpin bends in this ill-used vehicle; it has evidently given good service. The three men talk and laugh, as at a party, with rolls handed round and music roaring.

Another sudden stop, another exit; the African makes another dash – now for a pharmacy. We three in the back wait; more of the driver's sorrys and our patient *maalesh*.² I wonder at the African's mission. Is he charged with some service? Is he sick? He didn't seem so. A condom perhaps? Or a medicine with morphine? Dark thoughts, I own.

He's coming back now, but I don't know what's in the packet he's holding to his chest – and I can't ask. The woman next to me smiles – a knowing one – but I am perplexed.

A little way and the woman waves that she wants to get out; she walks off with her tonnage without a word.

A little way more and we pass the old family house at Kornet Chehwan, derelict, out of service.

Thérèse hands notes to our merry driver; we get out awkwardly with our parcels. The three men drive on to music, sandwiches, medicine and high spirits. In their shared taxi they pass the open service station on the road up to Bikfaya.

We walk with our parcels down towards the church at Ain Aar; it is too late for the evening service.

---

¹ *hamdullah – thank God*
² *maalesh – it doesn't matter*

2010

Search after Hitchcock

We are lost on our way to a theatre in Jounieh, my daughter, fresh from college, driving. We pull up at a petrol station on the *autostrade*. In fluent Arabic, she asks the attendant the way. He's a foreign worker from Egypt and doesn't know. At the other pump there's a grey automobile, shiny with big fins; it's long and capacious, made before power steering. The attendant asks the driver to speak to us. He is grey-suited with a thin tie, his black hair swept back – a suave match for his immaculate car. He speaks to us at the window in salesman English – like a man who knows too much – and I wonder if he is the wrong man to ask. Trusting him, despite a queasy suspicion, he bids us follow to the theatre. We see him open his ample door, slide in and sit at the huge wheel; there is no seat-belt. He pulls away from the gas station with us in ropeless tow. We follow him off the highway, his raised fins bright with light, signaling left and right, swerve into dim thoroughfares, rough roads, onto treacherous unsigned bends. I look through the rear window to see if we are trailed, but no notorious gangster tracks us. I am spellbound by this blind chase, as though our man in his automobile had no shadow of a doubt about our destination, my daughter driving on, young and innocent. To me it seems like vertiginous pursuit, as uncanny as spellbound Scottie driven to follow his fatal blonde on 'Frisco's steep streets. Now we've hit the highway again as though to make the ring. I go by my compass – we're heading north by northwest – feel myself sweating in a frenzy to reach our theatre. My daughter thinks it rich and strange, this weaving in and out like restless birds, but I, at this late stage, confess to fright. And now our guide's brazen light is winking – he's pulling in and there's a crowd outside – *hamdullah!*[1] – we've reached the theatre. He sees us as we pass, like strangers on a train. We wave our thanks and descend slowly into a dark car park.

In the foyer, with the start of the performance running one-hour-Lebanese late, I glimpse a portly form – no secret agent this – but Alfred, among the theatregoers, in characteristic cameo part.

[1] *hamdullah! – thank God!*

Embedded in the narrative are eighteen titles of films directed by Alfred Hitchcock.

2011

Washing Ill-Temper Away

Driving back from Broumanna on a blue February morning, mountain snow melting, my foot hits the left pedal. I let the blackguard driver out from a church car park, his rear lights fluttering onto the bending road. He stops to pick up a passenger. Irritation from behind – hoot, hoot. I sit firm at the wheel. Wait. Continuous hooooooot. With tense look in rear mirror, I see arms waving impatience. Culprit car drifts slowly forward – then shoots off. I change from N to D, let off handbrake, put foot to right pedal – hear hoots of anger as the one behind flies by. I am rattled and tail him. I'm not to be diminished by his temper …. *Hear the words of the mystic Rumi, mind sent into dervish whirl: the fault you see in another, you will find in yourself* … We reach *rond point*,[1] he right to Bikfaya and I left onto the highway down. When I arrive home, my wife tells me she has an appointment to have her hair done – would I drive her? We start arguing, splitting unnecessary hairs …. *the mirror reflects your face. Do not strike at the mirror, O Hasan. Stars cast their image on water. Why throw dirt at them? They may seem to disappear, but they have not gone out ….* I drive my wife to the salon to take out the grey, time for my dark mood to pass before she sets off for her remote cousin's funeral …. *Therefore, wash ill-temper away.*

---

[1] *rond point (French) – roundabout*

2011

Permit, Passport, Parking

I am a foreigner. My wife is not. I have applied for a permit to stay. We are going to the Ministry to pick up my passport. Permission has been weeks in slow process and tomorrow I am booked on a flight.

The building is somewhere in Beirut – a Lebanese labyrinth. I drive through districts unknown, meet with hoots of irritation and impatience, gestures of fury – brace myself and nose a way through cars, bumper to bumper, cut a gap into the clogged roundabout – come near to scraping our well-scratched car.

Ministry finally found, I slot into a parking space left free by a car departing. We are fortunate, for vehicles here stifle street space and air; unfortunate when told my passport cannot be returned: the permit will take more time. My papers will be sent to a branch for identity check. All hope gone now for flight next morning – too late to postpone or cancel for refund.

We walk back to our car. Three policemen are chatting, one leaning on the bonnet, pad and pen in hand. He is about to write us a ticket.

Policeman: *Parking is not permitted here.*

Thérèse (protesting): *We took the space of a car departing.*

Policeman: *Would you copy someone about to commit suicide?*

He puts away his pad and lets us off. I drive into the maelstrom of the metropolis. Without permit or passport, I feel like a person with no name or state.

*   *   *

Two bad-tempered days have gone by since our futile visit to the Ministry. But now we are descending the stairs of another government office – jubilant. I have my stamped passport in one hand and a residence permit – valid for three years in the shape of a plastic card – in my other hand. But foreign husband and Lebanese wife have not gone far in search of their parked car when they hear a loud crackling sound coming from a building on the other side of the road. Our attention is drawn to a group of men standing on a flat roof.

"Sounds like a celebration with fireworks," I say. "Perhaps someone has finally had their passport stamped and returned by the authorities."

"No," Thérèse corrects me. "They're not fireworks, but gunshots. Can't you see them firing into the air?"

See thenationalnews.com/mena/lebanon/2021/12/30/a-booming-market-lebanese-rush-to-buy-weapons-for-personal-security

2012

Down South

David is a Ph.D. student at the American University of Beirut. His mother and father have come from Boston, in the United States, to visit him. David has made friends with a member of the office staff, Nour, who works in the Archives Department on the campus; she has invited him and his parents to lunch at her village near Nabatieh, though the taxi is running late and has yet to appear. I am chatting with Tom, David's father. David and his mother, Alison, have bought sandwiches and drinks to take with us for breakfast on the road to Saida and the south.

The taxi arrives and we bundle in with our rucksacks. The driver, who introduces himself as Toufic, speaks some English; he explains his lateness:

"My wife is sick," he says. "The pharmacy no medication. Must go to other."

The taxi approaches downtown Beirut and joins the Airport *autostrade*. The traffic is heavy but fast-moving – too fast!

We pass Damour and are now arriving at Saida. Here we leave Toufic, who will go in search of the medication he needs for his wife, while we take another taxi for the climb up to Nabatieh. The grass is green with spring beside the winding road; village streets are narrow; vistas open up to mountains – the air is clean.

At Nabatieh, we are met by a young man, Nour's brother, Ali. He drives us in a large pickup truck to his village. We pass a mosque, and then a church, before reaching the house of Nour's family – her husband, their two young children and Nour's old mother. We sit down to eat *mloukhia*.[1] It tastes just as Marie, my mother-in-law, would make it. The children look at us shyly as we eat. We converse with Nour and her husband. They do not speak of politics, but rather of cultivating the land. Nour's old mother sits and eats in silence. When the meal ends, Ali joins us for coffee. He is going to take us to see an old Crusader fortification.

The ruins of Beaufort Castle, known locally as *Kalaat Cheiif*,[2] stand three-hundred metres high on a cliff. From there we look down at the Litani River and beyond to forests. Ali points to the disputed Shebaa Farms, Haramoun's white heights, the green of the Houleh plain, and to the west, the glitter of the sea. Before us lie three countries, though we see no borders. The Crusader lords of Sidon built Beaufort Castle, but Saladin the Victorious drove them out. Then came the Ottoman's and overran the fortress with imperial power. They assigned the Shiite Sa'b family caretakers of the castle, until the Druze emir of the Shouf mountains, took it back, he being later ousted and executed by the affronted Ottomans, they reinvesting the Sa'bs to the ruined castle. Fast forward to modern times: those from Palestine exiled from their land, occupation in Lebanon's south; Beaufort Castle a strategic point to rain down shells on Israel's troops in Galilee. The enemy retaliates and occupies the castle, base for war operations in Lebanon's north. The pile is left mutilated after troop withdrawal, time now for current renovation under the benefit of Lebanon's peace.

David, Tom, Alison, Ali and I are in a full bus bumping its way round hairpin bends to another tourist destination. As we pass through a village, three young men in front take in admiring views of girls not wearing *hijab*.[3] Ali hears one say, "Why did Allah make women so beautiful if we are not meant to admire them?" He translates these wise words for us to dwell on.

The bus has arrived at the Hezbollah War Museum atop oak-and-birch-covered Mleeta Mountain. Ali points to nearby villages: Habboush, Jargou', Jbaa', Mleekh, Al-Luwaiza, Ain Buswar – and way beyond to the fractious southern border. On foot, we enter the museum and pass through a concrete arch towards the main square where visitors are assembled. Ali introduces us to our guide – Hassan; his English is fluent.

"I shall take you first to the Exhibition," he says. "There you will find captured equipment, spoils of war, and descriptions of Israel's army and their leaders, who occupied the south of our country for twenty years until we forced them to retreat." ...

... We are at "The Abyss" where lies an open landscape punctuated by enemy weaponry: tanks, bullets, shells, helmets. And at its centre, next to a tombstone, a once-powerful Israeli Mirkava-4 Tank, immobilised, sunk half-way into the earth....

... Where the resistance fighters planned their strategy is named "The Pathway". Inside a camouflaged barricade are Hezbollah's armaments and equipment: Kalashnikovs on display, ammunition, helmets, backpacks, jackets. Further along, entrenchments, barricades and bunkers lead on to "The Cave", hacked out of the mountain, where the fighters lived through the heat of summer and the cold winds of winter. Hassan points to cots and kitchenware, to an electrical generator and to office telephones, radios and computers....

... Our guide leads us out onto a balcony – "The Outlook" – where trees grow on all sides. Alison takes photographs, Tom studies his guide book, David talks to Hassan in the Arabic he has learned living in the crowded suburb of Dowra; I survey the landscape....

... Lastly to "The Line of Fire" and Hezbollah's military hardware. From here the freedom fighters looked down on Israeli army outposts – and fired at them until the enemy, fatigued, turned tail and retreated to their own frontier. Hassan tells us this with pride. I hear David say, "This war museum is like the ones we have in America."

I mutter, "Would that there were no more wars" – and recalling our passing through the village, "Better to worship the beauty of women than praise the wars of men."

Hassan nods in assent. "There are plans to make this site into a tourist area," he says with enthusiasm. "There will be swimming pools, a spa, playgrounds, hotels and a camping area, and even a cable car to the nearby town of Sojod. That will be when we live in peace with our neighbours."

[1] *mloukhia: rice, spinach and meat (chicken, beef or lamb), onions in vinegar added with pieces of toasted Lebanese bread sprinkled on top.*
[2] *Kalaat – castle in Arabic; Cheiif – high rock in old Aramaic*
[3] *hijab – headscarf*

2013

Bekaa's Bounty

Passing through Kab Elias you see mosques, one not yet finished with spindly minarets. Then comes a straight road lined by tall poplars, reminiscent of Napoleon's ways. The landscape opens out to rising mountain slopes to the right, littered with new villas. To your left, the flat valley stretches away to the Anti-Lebanon heights.

> *This land is richly cultivated:*
> *dark soil begets*
> *sweet corn, cucumber, cabbage,*
> *bulbous onions and fat potatoes*
> *some destined for the crisp factory.*
> *The wheat fields have been reaped;*
> *cherries picked;*
> *apples, pears, plums, and peaches proliferate;*
> *the vine is ready to yield its juice*
> *for aniseed tasting arak*
> *and for wine – red, white and rosé.*
> *Olives await autumn to be plucked.*

When you cross the mountains to Syria beyond, such bounty is hardly believable, so lacking in water is the land.

2014

Cold Fruit

The four of us set off, in the mid-morning, for Ferzol, a village near Zahle in the Bekaa Valley: Yammine, my father-in-law, Thérèse and I, with Michel, her brother, at the wheel. The sun was winter-weak; rain had come down the day before and there was first December snow on the high mountain slopes. It became colder inside the car as we ascended and crossed the pass; I was glad of the layers of clothes I had put on before leaving.

In Zahle, Michel pulled in at a roadside greengrocer. The shop was not on the sunny side of the street; the cold struck me as I got out of the car. In the open air, bananas hung from an iron beam in huge clumps; oranges, lemons and clementines, displayed in sloping boxes, lined the raised forecourt; carrots, cucumber – large and small – potatoes with Bekaa Valley soil on them, onions, aubergines, hanging garlic bundles, plump lettuce, large tomatoes, bunches of parsley and boxed dates. With the remaining warmth evaporating from my body, I could see such abundance lasting a long time in these frigid conditions.

Yammine spent some time choosing fruit for the family we were going to visit in Ferzol. Thérèse also took her time. Michel sat in the car and I, feeling the cold creeping up my legs, joined him. From inside, I could see Yammine, head down, inspecting the fruit and selecting with a close eye. In younger days he had once tended his own orchard. Thérèse too roamed around the shop as though the cold were of no concern of hers.

Having at last made their purchases, Thérèse helped her father step down from the forecourt. Michel got quickly out of the car to open up at the back for the fruit to be put in by a Syrian helper – and when the hatch was opened, a blast of cold air caught me. At that moment, I dreaded that the house we were to visit, where we would be sitting in conversation, would feel as cold as it did inside the car, for my experience of Lebanon's concrete blocks was that they held little heat.

I need not have worried. The room was small, the carpets thick, the air warmed by a glistening diesel stove. A kettle, exuding steam, sat on the hotplate. Any further warmth that may have been needed would have been supplied by the body heat of the three women and five men sitting in the room. We drank hot coffee and ate cold fruit – sliced bananas, laid out on plates, and oranges, peeled with segments parted. After family news and exchange of political opinion, there was talk of farm and domestic matters: the months taken pruning leaves from the large vineyard, the bottling of fig to make jam; cucumber and *me'te*[1] pickled; *labneh*[2] rolled into balls and jarred in olive oil – all these to be kept in a cool larder. And I thought: *these people have not lost touch with the land.*

With the afternoon advancing, the men went outside into the yard to load up the one-kilo sacks of *kishk*[3] Yammine had ordered – thirty of them in the back of the car. Job done and a wad of notes exchanged, the women came out to wave a long goodbye.

In Zahle, we stopped to eat – not fruit but wrapped *tawouk* chicken.[4] Unlike the farmhouse room we had been sitting in, the door of the restaurant remained wide open. There was also an arch leading onto a platform of tables and chairs by the roadside; it too was open. The moment we stepped into the restaurant I realised that it was going to be a cold repast.

*   *   *

We had seen the old man parked on a sharp bend with his van of apples on our way up to the pass. He was still there on our return descent. Michel pulled over and the four of us got out of the car. The slanting rays of the sun gave out no warmth; a wind blowing from the slope above pierced us. As Yammine, Thérèse and Michel took a look at the boxes of apples before choosing some to purchase, I thought of the old man huddled in his van all day with the doors open, displaying his fruit in the mountain cold, until in the late light he would drive away, only to return next day....

... It was almost dark when we stopped to fill up. The petrol station, attended by a wrapped up South Asian and a dog tethered to a chain, was dimly lit. I got out of the car in the hope of finding a toilet. In the low light, I could discern the arc of a Christmas crib set back from the road. I came close; it was as I had seen it before: shepherds facing Joseph and Mary, their gaze on the warm fruit of the Holy Mother's womb. And I wondered how cold it had been that night in the stable beyond Lebanon's heights.

---

[1] *me'te* – *similar to a cucumber but with a rough skin*
[2] *labneh* – *A soft cheese made from salted strained yogurt*
[3] *kishk* – *made from drained yogurt, or drained sour milk, and dried into powder for cooking*
[4] *tawouk* – *grilled marinated chicken breast*

2014

Christmas Nuggets

It's my seventy-seventh birthday and my daughter has gone shopping at *Le Mall*. I am waiting at McDoe's with a finished sundae cup in my hand; it's plastic and sticky. My watch advances slowly; I stare at the Christmas glitter, at Santa in a shop window, the tall light-bedecked tree, a reindeer tethered to a sleigh.

A woman with her daughter and two South Asians – maids perhaps, though they seem to be treated as equals – sit at my long table.

The maids eat with happy faces. Is this an off-duty treat, I wonder; Madame's Christmas outing? She picks at her chips but doesn't open her box.

The four of them take their time talking, while I sit hour-long with cup in hand pretending to be a long-standing customer. Madame glances at me. She must see that I do not look festive-happy with my unshaven face and tired demeanour – the result of a too-late night.

Food finished, except for unopened box, they eye me as they get up to leave. I've had enough of the Bangladeshi table cleaner hanging over me for my empty cup. I stand too. The woman turns to me, holding out her box, and says, "Would you like these chicken nuggets? – please take them."

I am in no mood for such delicacies and decline with an apologetic look – Madame takes away her box.

I wonder at her offer: not a Christmas gift, surely; nor can she know of my birthday. Did she think me hungry – an old codger eking out time with ice cream eaten? Ah, yes, she must think I am a refugee escaped across the border, come to Lebanon for fast food sanctuary.

Suddenly, I feel regret at not taking those Christmas nuggets; they seem like gold.

2014

A Maid Looks into a Mirror

The maid stops her dusting and stares into Madame's mirror; she remembers how she looked when first coming to this foreign country.
*Dark skin soft
with a slight shine
breasts budding
hair curly and thick
face firm
eyes alustre.*
She was a maiden then, full of hope for customary marriage. But her father had not given her away to a suitor, for he had drowned off the coast of Libya trying to cross the sea in a quest for paid employment. The maiden's mother could raise no dowry, she being left close to destitution; could only offer up her daughter to a far-away Levantine family to be taken on as serving maid.
She looks at her image in the mirror and sees herself as she is now—
*dark skin matte-
dry, cracked,
breasts pendulous
hair scalp-thin
face time-worn
eyes lack-lustre*
The children she has nurtured from birth will never be her own; the house she has lived in never her home, nor the mirror she faces.

2015

Slow Coach

We are on our way, Thérèse and I, to Quaker Meeting at Broumanna. Clouds drop April rain. We pick up the bus at Bikfaya and sit on hard seats behind a broad-shouldered driver who, before starting, leans on the wheel. Mounted next to him, a woman, housewifely, looking happy with a full view. The engine's turned on, the bus edges forward. I look at my watch; we have time.

There's a stop at a bend. The motor goes silent. Rain patters on the roof. A passenger dismounts; he will purchase morning *manouche*.[1] We others - Thérèse and I, young men from Egypt released for Sunday, church-bound Ethiopian maid, woman up front, sit waiting for the *manouche* man.... The driver blows a warning horn and turns the key to start. The man comes running, packet in hand, jumps aboard at the back door. The bus rolls forward down a slope, engine jerking in slow motion, driver changing into third.

Slow, low gears to Baabdat. There's someone standing in the rain. His unsmart looks tell me he's a refugee from Syria. He gesticulates; the driver seems to understand, stops and turns the motor off. The man crosses the slippery road and disappears down steps .... We wait .... see him appear again with two others – compatriots – father, tall, holding baby, blanket-wrapped against the rain, and mother clinging to her wind-swept scarf. They take refuge in the waiting bus. I look at my watch and see the hands have advanced ...

... The hands have advanced and the bus stands still. The hungry driver has pulled in to pick up a late breakfast at a roadside place. Back in the cab, we catch the woody smell of hot *zartar*[2] and are warmed by it. He eats at the wheel and, when finished, lights a smoky fag – it makes Thérèse cough and she protests at a lamentable lack of motion. He shrugs broad shoulders and makes exchanges with the woman to his right – the one who sees it all through the wiped windscreen ...

... On the slow road again, he is phoning on his loud mobile to the driver of the bus ahead; it is out of sight and he's trying not to catch up. We see little women from the Philippines waiting as the bus halts. When the door hisses open, they clamber up, glistening wet. You hear their Sunday chatter as they fold their umbrellas and settle into their seats. The woman sitting by the driver plays her part. She pulls down a lever and the door hisses closed.

We are nearing school gates. I ask the driver for *madrasa*.[3] He's perplexed by my anglo-accent until Thérèse cuts in. The bus stops, but the wipers don't cease their urgent oscillations. Thérèse is fumbling for money in her assorted bag – she can't find the notes. Broad shoulders turn with impatience. The door is still shut and I'm eager to get out.

The driver: "You want to waste my time, Madame?"

Thérèse, scorching: "You have wasted OUR time!"

The money's found and slapped into the driver's hand. The lever's pushed up and we descend into the deluge. I feel we've been taken for a ride.

---

[1] *manouche: a flat bread topped with thyme, cheese or finely ground minced meat*
[2] *zartar – thyme*
[3] *madrasa – school*

2015

Teta Marie's Walk

My mother-in-law, *Teta*[1] Marie Karim Yammine, and I used to spend quite a lot of time together. I would visit her each morning for coffee in the flat where she lived opposite us in the family building. Thérèse, and other family members, would often join us. I was curious to know more about Marie's life before she married; but because she did not speak English, nor I Arabic, I needed an interpreter to help gather up her story. This role was to be taken on by Thérèse.

Over a period of several weeks, I put questions to Marie and she would come back with descriptions of her youth in pre-independent Lebanon. This left me to piece together her family history in the form of a written narrative. Since it is probable that most of the extended family knew little about Marie's early life, I am glad that there is now a record of those years by which Marie can be remembered, particularly because in 2016 she passed away.

*   *   *

She was a girl in those Second-World-War days when France had fallen; but still the "Free French" governed and would not let go of little Lebanon.

Marie was fifteen years old when she went to work at Jraidini's stocking and laundry factory. Each day, save Sunday, she would walk the coast road with three or four of her sisters from her home in Antelias to the factory at Dowra – a long way there in the morning and a long way back in the evening.

All day she stood at loud electric machines, along with her kin and a hundred others, making and repairing men's socks and women's nylon stockings. It was Adèle, her eldest sister, who had charge of seventy women and girls.

In winter the walk was often rainy; the girls would arrive home with cold wet feet in saturated shoes. They would dry out beside the open charcoal burner, lit and stoked up by their mother, she who had given birth to six daughters and a son – those who had not miscarried – before she died at fifty-five.

The house possessed a fertile garden from which the family gained healthy sustenance. With buckets in hand, the girls would gather in from the earth – potatoes, lettuce, beans, carrots, and onions – passing them on for preparation in their mother's kitchen. They picked parsley, mint and thyme, and in winter, lemons and oranges; in summer, dates, apricots, plums and quince, some to be jarred as jam; in autumn they harvested figs from the tree before the birds could eat them, grapes from straggling vine, and olives to be preserved and eaten with *labneh*.[2]

On occasion, a lamb or sheep was killed and cooked whole on a wood fire kindled from spiky pine, and, after repast, the left-over meat mixed with animal fat to be preserved for the winter. Later, chickens, roaming free, laid their eggs generously in this natural garden, giving further family nourishment.

Marie's father, with *tarboosh*[3] on head, brought home sacks of flour in a cart; the women made bread on the *saj*[4] and ate fully, while those in want came close to starving. His donkey pulled the cart, the cart carried supplies; the father worked as hard as his donkey, carting and selling, collecting junk, building houses, letting flats – and grew rich. His brother, his partner, prospered too and purchased a smart car in those uncrowded days. But Marie's father carried on with his donkey and grew richer. Eschewing banks and lenders, he hid his gains in the house above a metal beam. He died with money on his mind. On his deathbed he is said to have held up a bank note and uttered: "The lira has flown!" He passed on, leaving his fortune behind. Inheritance went to the single son, the girls left to the fortune of spouses when they came.

For eight years Marie walked the road from Antelias to Jraidini's factory – without a stop, except on the day French warships shelled the capital, and oil and gas tanks were dispatched in flames. With President, Prime Minister, and Chamber deputies imprisoned, there were protests in town, and people and politicians cried out, "Down with Hitler and out with the French!" Then little Lebanon's Cedar flag was raised.

On that big occasion in 1944, Jraidini's factory was closed for the day and the girls sent home. The time had come for Marie to plan her own home trade: repairs to Lebanon's denizens' laddered stockings and old, holed socks. She could then profit and take the bus to town to buy herself a pretty frock.

---

[1] *Teta* – Grandmother
[2] *labneh* – a soft cheese made by straining the liquid from yogurt
[3] *tarboosh* – a man's round hat made of red felt with a black tassel at the top
[4] *saj* – a large, flat, convex-shaped cooking device for baking flat bread

2016

Three Sisters

My wife, Thérèse, and her two sisters, Saidi and Hannah, were French-educated, as is common among Christians in Lebanon. Unlike their mother and father, who spoke only Arabic, I was able to communicate with the two younger sisters in the French language.

On one occasion when the family were breakfasting together at Ain Aar, I asked Saidi how the sisters had got on in their younger days at Kornet Chehwan. All eyes turned to Thérèse, all faces smiling. It seemed that Thérèse had not conformed to a traditional domestic role as would have been expected of a girl soon to become a woman – and Saidi and Hannah began reminiscing about how the sisters would share their tasks on cleaning day. Their "story" gave rise to a good deal of laughter. It called out to be written down.

* * *

Thérèse used to read books and bury herself in them. She would engage with the European classics – Flaubert and Zola, Chekhov and Dickens – whenever she could, which meant that she had to find a quiet spot away from her sisters and two brothers.

Since space was short at home in this large family, she would hitch herself up with both legs pressed against the wall of the corridor, rest above the door and read; or climb the big fig tree outside their house in Kornet Chehwan and find peace among singing birds.

Saidi, or Sousou as she was called, was more the housekeeping sort. She would put things in their proper place, clean ashtrays after use, puff up sofa cushions when they had been sat on, and make sure that all was spotless in the family home.

Hannah, the youngest, was still not in her teens, but she would assist when her mother was cooking or needed help with washing the dishes, or wet clothes had to be hung on the line.

Saturday was house-cleaning day. All three girls would gather up dusters, brooms, brushes, mops, cloths – clean windows, polish furniture, sweep floors, and dust all over. Little Hannah would wipe the tiles in the kitchen while Sousou scrubbed the floor; but Thérèse had a way of disappearing, she not being disposed to household chores, but rather to learning and a life of the imagination.

"Where is Thérèse?" asked Sousou with duster in hand and sweat on her forehead. "Have you seen her, Hannah?"

She had not; nor had her mother and brothers. They called out but received no reply. They looked in the garden; she was not there. Was she in the road cleaning their father's car? No! The sisters started searching – in cupboards, in cubbyholes, in corners, but did not find her.

"Perhaps she's so tired she's sleeping somewhere," Hannah surmised, and went into their bedroom followed by her elder sister.

On the floor Sousou espied a shoe. "Isn't that Thérèse's?"

"Yes," said Hannah and pulled up the bedcover. "That's Thérèse's leg!"

"And there she is under the bed. What are you doing there, sister? We were looking for you all over."

Thérèse didn't answer but appeared holding a bulky tome.

"Reading, were you?" Sousou said, annoyed.

"Yes."

"Wasting time!"

Thérèse remained silent.
"What were you reading?"
"A novel."
"What novel, pray?"
"*À la recherche du temps perdu.*"

À la recherche du temps perdu, *the novel by Marcel Proust, has been translated in the English edition as* Remembrance of Things Past; *but it could be translated as "in search of lost time."*

2016

Among the Classics

My book, the first to be published, is on sale in the bookshops of Lebanon. It is a volume of poems written during our time in Kuwait, with the sun rising on the front cover, taken by my daughter. This is designed as an emblem of the East, for it is a volume devoted to the cultures of the peoples of Asia, stretching from the Arab world to the Far East and India. These are *Poems of the East*.

Last Tuesday, Christina visited Antoine's bookshop at the ABC department store in Dbayeh, just to see if my book was on display. Yes, there it was, placed under "Local Authors."

"My father wrote this book," Christina tells the girl at the counter, who expresses naïve amazement. "But my father is not a local author; he's British." And, wanting to see the book given as much exposure as possible, she asks for another copy to be put on the "Poetry" shelves. The shop assistant, full of awe, agrees.

Yesterday, we visited Virgin Megastore in Ashrafieh. It's a big place selling books as well as DVDs. We couldn't find my book at first, then spotted it. There it was – *Poems of the East* by Antony Johae – surprisingly, I thought, placed next to Khalil Gibran's *The Prophet* on one side and William Shakespeare's *Othello* on the other – and, to my further amazement, accompanied by Rumi, Hafez, Rihani, Balzac, Beaudelaire, Emily Dickinson, Walt Whitman, the Bronte sisters, Jane Austen, Dickens, Dostoevsky, Dante, and Tolstoy – my book, *Poems of the East*, already among the "Classics"!

2017

Book Sale at Jbail

I am the owner of too many books: fiction, factual, criticism, biography, poetry, anthologies, textbooks, reference books and glossaries. In short, it is time for a cull. At Jbail, on some Saturdays, you can sell your books in a small public garden. This is appropriate, because Jbail's ancient Greek name was Byblos ...

It is afternoon. The winter sun is warm. A woman, whom I take to be the organiser, directs me to a table under a palm tree. The garden is quiet and my books lie untouched on the table; they are displayed according to type, some placed in piles; academic journals, assorted poetry pamphlets and magazines in a staggered row; a few fat reference books, a quantity of sprawling novels, some almost new, others well-fingered near to falling apart; the remainder a junk miscellany – and in a prominent place, ten copies of my *Poems of the East*.

The afternoon is advancing; the sun will soon be hidden behind the palm tree. I am waiting for purchasers to appear.... Garden lights are switched on. Families on evening promenade pass by my table without looking. They are not out for books.

A couple stop, we talk and when I tell them my poem, "Desert Flowers", is in this large (vanity) volume, they are impressed and make the first purchase.

Not long, and a lone man leans over the table to peer.

"Why are you selling these books?" he asks. I tell him I am a retired academic, that I own too many books, and rather than reading them, I am writing some lines on Lebanon.

"Where will you publish?"

"Here in Lebanon. My wife will translate these lines into Arabic and we'll publish a dual text."

The lone man shakes his head. "I am a lawyer. Let me tell you: you will be cheated. Go abroad. Find somebody there. Try Saqi in London."

He turns over a few volumes and selects *The Which Guide to Women's Health* (one of my wife's possessions. I wonder who the book is for, but do not ask). He pays the nominal one thousand liras, wishes me luck with publication and moves on.

Strollers go past – students perhaps, couples oblivious of books, husbands and wives keeping an eye on their roving children, an old man leaning on his walking stick, a pretty girl who hobbles on high-heels, clusters of laughing teenagers, flirting when a girl comes into sight. They hardly glance at my table. I catch the eye of a young woman at a stand opposite.

I call out: "Buy one, get one free!"

She comes over and begins perusing my stock, turning over each volume as though searching. She looks up at me and says, "Can you recommend a book?" – then corrects herself – "two books?"

"What kind of book – er, books?"

"Literary criticism."

I show her past issues of *New Comparison* piled twenty high, on sale for less than a dollar. She flips through several and chooses one.

"Will I get one free?" she asks rather timidly.

"Please have two free."

The young woman is clearly moved by this offer and pays hastily as though I were about to change my mind. I give her back four thousand liras in exchange for her five-thousand note. She settles the three volumes carefully into her holdall bag – but she doesn't leave. Her continued presence is attracting promenaders to my table – and my books are selling now that I have adopted a two-for-the-price-of one sales pitch.

"What is this?" the young woman asks holding up an A4 spiral monograph entitled *Five Forays into the Early Modern Age*.

I explain that it is a long essay published in a journal when I was teaching in the Gulf. "You are welcome to have it gratis."

The young woman is looking at the Table of Contents. "Can you tell me what it is about?" and insists I give a summary of each chapter.

My micro-lecture begins to attract an audience; I find the table surrounded and when I have finished with my resume of the last chapter, purchases take off spectacularly. But the original ten copies of my *Poems of the East* remain; they are not on offer for a thousand liras a piece, nor will fetch two for the price of one.

"May I have a word?"

It is the woman who allotted my table addressing me; she is distinguished-looking, with long black hair and wearing a smart two-piece suit.

"My name is Eliane; I am the organiser of this book sale."

I know enough Arabic to say "*Sharafna.*"[1]

"I am interested in your *Poems of the East*," she says picking up a copy. "Are they about Lebanon?"

I tell her there are some, while others cover my travels in the region and beyond.

"The thing is," she says, "our speaker has cancelled his talk at the last minute. Could you read some of your poems in the pavilion? I don't want to disappoint our audience; they are waiting."

My wife, daughter and son-in-law pack up my books, while I accompany Eliane to the pavilion – a sort of summer house in the garden – with ten copies of *Poems of the East* in my arms.

The audience becomes hushed as we enter. The house is full. Eliane offers apologies for the change of programme and I am left free to wax poetic about Lebanon's heights, Kuwait's old boats, a jaunt in Jordan and Egypt's flooding river. Audience applause and Eliane's thanks follow. Time for my listeners to approach, to ponder over and purchase *Poems of the East*.

At the evening's end, nine copies sold at fifteen dollars apiece – a book sale indeed! But I have not come to this garden for profit, rather to see my books reach good hands.

Now the pavilion door is shut; garden lights are switched off; the Jbail sale ended.

Part Three: Border Lines

2017

Storm

We are three abreast, Thérèse, Christina, and I, on a flight to Istanbul, final destination Beirut. We are soon to land, when the captain speaks on the intercom – there is bad weather over the city; we must fly on to Ankara, thirty minutes distant.

The seat-belt sign lights up. I look out from my window; the sky has turned murky dark; I have not seen such clouds – there is anger in them and we are flying their way. Lights in the cabin are set low as the first bumps hit, the plane pitches and I grab the seat arm. A woman with a sleeping girl on her lap begins to moan. The plane lurches to one side, wing dipping. The woman's moans are drenched in fear; they send contagion. I want her to stop – to be quiet as the child sleeps on. The father holds a crying baby, speaks anxious words in Turkish.

The plane plunges, leaving my inside behind. I picture the pilot's hands wrestling with the clouds. A few rows in front of us two men are chatting in a merry English, their guffaws loud, as though no battle with the sky were in progress – is this Anglo-Saxon cover for anxiety? The other passengers are quiet, but not the moaning woman; she will not let up, nor the crying baby.

This plane's name is *Pegasus*, divine winged stallion, friend of the Muses. It gives momentary heart in the commotion, before taking a dive. I wonder at the engine's horsepower.

I do not think of Thérèse in the aisle seat – my wife. It is as though our customary holding hands on take-off and touch-down were bereft of meaning, my daughter's hand in mine, mere sweat. I feel only a terrible turbulence, dreading it might be my last in the falling and soaring, with an end in exile on the stallion's constellation.[1]

Body buffeted, the wing rising, falters, shudders like a shivering swimmer. I suffer the strain; hope it will hold. The moaning woman thinks not. From their laughter, the Englishmen think nothing of it. Now it is night-dark outside, tinged yellow as though the aircraft were penetrating a sick sky. I imagine our falling into a black sea.

---

[1] *In Greek mythology, Zeus transformed Pegasus into one of the eighty-eight constellations in space.*

2018

In a Mountain Village

Once, there were only a few hundred inhabitants here; they lived in stone-built cottages, drew water from a spring, cultivated the mountainsides, despatched fruit and vegetables by donkey and cart to the town below, or sold to travellers on their way up to the pass. They kept cattle and flocks which they took to market or slaughtered, cooked and consumed on special feast days.

But the coming of the automobile changed their ways; the villagers sold their rich soil to city dwellers; this allowed the villagers to send their offspring to get an education at the universities springing up on the coastal strip; the graduates did not come back to live in the village.

Those city dwellers who had purchased land, built mansions on generous plots from money gained through the craft of business, sometimes made in foreign places, or perhaps by local politicians whose fortunes rest on stealth. Others invested in high apartment blocks to be sold at sky-high prices – posh piles built to be occupied solely in the summer when temperatures in towns at sea level rise to stifling heat and the cool of mountain elevation offers sanctuary.

In the cold season, these "residences" and "high-end deluxe" new blocks remain uninhabited, save for Syrian workers who wait for their caretaker wages and the coming of the owners' seasonal family and guests. Apartment windows and balcony doors are closed; shutters down. Only when raised can one surmise a resident installed for all seasons.

On a spring morning, one may observe an old man holding a shepherd's staff to the ground. He tends shaggy sheep and long-haired goats that chew fresh roadside grass, or grasp budding branches, or butt in play with their horns. At the sight of this flock and the old man with his staff, one is taken back to the village as it was before the internal combustion engine held sway, technology cut out mountain sites to build on, and modern edifices crowded the land.

This place is a village no longer, but rather a ghost suburb; its streets and roads are wide and empty, its moving cars occasional. Only in summer, when city people, tourists and expatriates take up temporary residence, does this village, that once was, take on life.

2018

Shoes

As I prepare for my walk and tie a shredding lace in a double knot, I note the condition of my shoes. They have travelled countless kilometres along El Metn's steep slopes and on roads worn out by countless cars. They will shortly be laid to rest, my shoes, outside the nuns' gate.

Walking down to Beit el Kikko, I feel them familiar, comfortable, like two firm friends. A smiling man hails me, one who works on a half-finished house.

"I am Syrian," he says. We talk – part simple Arabic, part simple English – he looking down at my feet. "You have good shoes – strong!"

Although they are attached to me, we shall soon have to be parted. To him, perhaps a refugee, these shoes look new, they having been polished, not paint-splattered like his thin plimsolls.

At home, I undo the double knots, pull off each shoe, and wipe them clean. I recall the Syrian's admiration for my sorry shoes. In a sudden flash, I understand what he was thinking: "This man's shoes are old. Maybe he will give them to me."

I put them in a plastic bag – like lovers, face-to-face – and carry them with me on my next El Kikko walk.

When I reach the building site, the Syrian and his workmates are not there. I think perhaps they have been called away on another job.

And so it was the next day and the next – half-built house abandoned. Now my shoes rest, retired, on the rack waiting for the Syrian's return.

2018

Exchanges

One Sunday, after Quaker Meeting, I get on the bus from Broumanna to Bikfaya. On the front seat, by the open door, a local woman, bare-shouldered but for black straps and straight fair hair down to her back.

On the other side, a couple, likely refugees, he dressed for summer, she with baby in arms, covered to her ankles. Baby kicks and babbles; mother babbles too.

With white arms stretched out, the woman by the door takes the baby to her white chest, rocks in silent lullaby; the baby's eyes flutter shut.

At Baabdat, she stands to get off. Mother takes back her sleeping baby with thanks to the local lady. Husband and wife smile, door shuts and the bus drives on.

2019

On the Eco-Road

The way to Saida is not beautiful. From the capital, a high wall masks the airport, graffiti marking it. Going south, the outlook is sullen with industry, the land chock-a-block. From the car you see beaches, litter-covered, and a high pile of waste before reaching the football stadium.

The way to Nabatieh is up between high hills and human habitation, through to its bannered streets and orphanage. The troupe unloads speakers, scenery, props and costumes. This will be a tale of refuse restored – plastic, metal, and paper – to three marked bins. A didactic piece designed to please.

The bins are placed on stage, set against sea, sky, ship and tree; the auditorium is a mass of kids. They smile at dancing dolphins, prancing turtles; shout at pestilential flies, bothersome bugs, biting mosquitoes; laugh at Wajih's wit[1], or lack of it; jump at Lina's screams; point frantically to pirates hiding in the wings; and, come grand finale, witness rubbish mountain packed into bins ready to be shaped again at factory, mill or workshop. The curtain is then drawn on an urgent eco-story.

Theatre lights are now out, orphans gone.

In the yard, the troupe loads speakers, scenery, props and costumes, ready to set off in car-and-van cavalcade. I find three bins and, about to put my coffee cup in the one marked *Plastic,* lift the lid and see assorted sweet papers, crusts of bread, and crisp packets aplenty. *Paper* is a similar mix, plus plastic cups – and *Metal* is anything but – to the brim. We'll not grin at this misdemeanour, nor despair, but like modern troubadours, continue on our eco-way.

[1] For Nazih Youssef, my son-in-law and his troupe of actors. Nazih it is who plays the part of Wajih. He is well known in the Arab world for his television sitcom comic role, and for his appearances in numerous films and theatre productions. He is much loved by the Lebanese public for his warmth and humour. In his television role as Wajih, Nazih has offered welcome light relief to local audiences in troubled economic times.

2019

Salon Smells

Thérèse and I were looking for the beauty salon. A taxi had dropped us off on a street corner in Jdeideh and we were now trudging our way along the pavement when it wasn't blocked by tilting parked cars.

We thought we had found it when, from a distance, bright shop lights came into view; but it turned out not to be the one where Thérèse had an appointment. She recalled that, previously, the taxi had taken the second turning after the Dowra flyover, whereas this time it had left us at the first turning.

It was winter-dark by now – and cold. The road leading to the second turning was lit only by the headlights of heavy traffic. We clung to the side of the road with cars passing from behind. I could hardly breathe the exhaust-filled air, though it didn't bother Thérèse.

When we turned the corner, the street seemed an unlikely place for a beauty salon; one side of the road was lined with parked lorries and, on the other, there were several decrepit-looking vans and a rusty caterpillar. There must have been a pile of uncollected rubbish nearby, because a smell of refuse grew stronger as we approached low lights coming from a shop window. Thérèse immediately recognized this as the place we had been searching for.

Inside the white-painted room the smells were inviting: shampoo and Eau de Cologne intermingled with cigarette smoke and the tang of coffee. It felt cosily warm as I sat on the sofa and waited for Thérèse to have her nails painted in an adjoining cubicle. To my right, on a raised platform, a large-bottomed woman, in tight black pants, leaned her head over a basin. A young man, who could still have been in his teens, rinsed the woman's hair a violent red; an unfamiliar odour filled the room. Another young man, with fashionable rips and tears in his blue jeans, stood and watched, looking down distractedly at his mobile phone from time to time, to finger it.

Sitting to my left in a raised salon chair and draped in a cover, a woman with a rather square face had her hair sprayed by a short-haired man with a long black beard. Moisture hung over the woman like a mist; its fragrance spread. I caught her looking at me in the mirror; I did not look back because to have done so might have felt like an intrusion into feminine privacy. Instead, my eyes turned to the soundless television screen hanging on the wall above the mirror: to street protests in Tripoli, demonstrators in Sur, marches in Saida, studio interviews with politicians, smashed car windows in downtown Beirut, soldiers holding back crowds from the *autostrade* in Jounieh – my vision was blocked by a long-haired woman in a short skirt. Smiling, she offered me black coffee in a small cardboard cup. As I took a first hot sip, a woman, heavily made up wearing a thin white summer dress, came into the salon and sat next to me on the sofa. She fumbled through her handbag; I could smell perfume mixed with a faint whiff of leather. A balding unshaven middle-aged man, whom I took to be the salon proprietor, approached us; the woman stood up and spoke to him, then zipped-shut her handbag and left. In the same moment, a pretty girl with frizzy hair entered and was greeted by the woman in the short skirt who ushered her to a seat in the far corner of the room. A minute later, an aproned employee appeared from a side door. She sat down facing her client and zip-opened her kit; the pretty frizzy girl smiled as she waited for her manicure to begin. Not long, and I caught a waft of acetone ...

In the aura of this parlour, I drifted into reverie ...

I had dozed off when I heard a voice. My eyes opened. Thérèse stood in front of me with her hands outstretched.

"Do you like them?" she said showing off her wet white nails. I nodded sleepily.

"Are you all right?" she asked. "The people here were worried about you – they saw your head drooping; they thought something was wrong."

"Just enjoying the soporific salon smells," I replied and waited for her nails to dry.

2019

Water and Waste

Partway through my shower, the water dries up. *Ma fi mai* [1] is a regular cry – of resignation if you need to flush the pan, frustration if you want to freshen up, despair if the shampoo's on your head; the flow becomes a trickle, trickle becomes drips, and not a drop to rinse off the soap.

There's another national problem to do with keeping things clean: *sbeili* is the oft-reiterated word – rubbish – plastic bags of it piled beside the oily road. There are no more places to dump it and the politicians are out of ideas. It's being said that the piles are destined for Germany, but is this a fair exchange for glossy Mercedes? Be that as it may, the rubbish keeps rising – and the smell in the high summer sun!

The population is getting heated and some have taken to the streets in downtown Beirut. LBC, MTV, OTV, Al-Manar, Al-Jadeed, Future, NBN, and Tele Liban are making a drama of it; protesters gesticulate in anger; they air their views loudly. Some carry placards, moving them up and down to catch the camera's eye. A girl gives vigorous nods as a journalist commentates; she gets a word in here and there, her head popping up, puppet-like, in protest.

Young men roam the road; they throw rubbish at policemen assembled to disperse them. With helmets and shields, the force advances, lobbing teargas canisters into the crowd, dull retaliation for waste; it's enough to make you weep.

In the cloudy air, a tanker has appeared; hoses are unravelled and water sprayed on those who will not step back from the Parliament building. There is no verbal persuasion here, but cold jets poured on hot tempers and filthy streets.

I think of my bath and the drip-dripping of the faucet and wish I were out there among the demonstrators under a shower of water with the soap and dirt washing away. It wouldn't be a waste.

[1] *Ma fi mai – there's no water.*

2019

La débâcle se poursuit ...

After sultry summer comes the deluge; streets turn into rivers – houses, offices, international airport, the Ministry of Works, are feet in water; motorists caught in tunnels; shoppers marooned at malls; President confined to palace; politicians – in the downpour – powerless.

Picture a street in south Beirut, see Ouzai's shop fronts, their wares saturated, scattered, floating, or lost from sight in the murk; uncollected rubbish dispersed and carried away in the stream; red van, water above its wheels; white car, half-submerged, grill drinking in the flood.

But with Lebanese light heart, sullen clouds become bright play: witness kids, fascinated, splish-splashing; a figure ensconced in a green canoe, paddling; a man in a colourful cap, enthroned on a plastic chair, perched on a white surfboard, his companion standing, long pole in hand, pushing his passenger along the watery way.

Oh, what fun it is to play on a relentless rainy day!

2019

The Reservoir

Many rivers flow down from Lebanon's snowy heights into the Mediterranean Sea – Litani, Damour, Dog, Kadisha, Ibrahim and a dozen others – potential for hydro-electric power and constant water supply; but fresh water goes to waste in the salty sea and the rivers dry up when the summer sun beats down. Governments have proposed the construction of dams to form mountain reservoirs but have met with dissent from opposing political parties and from concerned naturalists. Thus flow the rivers unimpeded into the sea.

But here's a government minister who has taken matters into his own hands and set in train the building of a barrier on the coast by Batroun. The reservoir will not be fed by the flow of mountain streams but be filled when it deigns to rain ...

... but no rain came, or hardly any, and when it did, it was paltry and sank through the stony floor of the reservoir, leaving it empty. The Minister's project seemed to have failed – his popularity took a plunge. It was seen by the careworn population as yet another government failure.

Then came the harshest winter in four decades; snow covered Lebanon's slopes for months and the rain seemed hardly to stop, causing the residents of Batroun to shiver in the cold. But the Minister's reservoir was empty no more – it filled up.

Now spring has come; a general election is due, and the Minister expects soon to be elected, for has he not proved his sceptics wrong? Has he not fulfilled his plan with a full reservoir?

But one may ask, what will happen when the sun gathers its summer strength and the rain no longer falls? Will there still be water stored, or will it be sucked up by the sun or sink back into the soil?

No matter, for by then, the Minister will have retained his parliamentary seat.

2019/2021

Generator Joke

Here is a quotation from the internet dated 29th March 2019:

Lebanon has not had capacity to supply 24-hour electricity since its 1975-1990 civil war, leaving many households reliant on their own generators or private neighbourhood suppliers who charge hefty fees to keep a few lights on or other appliances running during regular daily cuts that can last several hours.

And again:

In March 2020, the crisis culminated in the country's first sovereign default. While electricity blackouts have been a persistent problem for decades, they became a full-blown crisis in the summer of 2021, when the Lebanese state failed to secure the foreign currency necessary to buy fuel.

To the internet question, "Is Lebanon still without electricity?" the answer is:

At present, the government supplies electricity for only one to three hours a day on average while people who can afford it supplement that supply with private generators. The public sector and private generator industry rely on polluting climate-intensive fossil fuels.

Other reports make it clear that the vast majority of the population cannot afford to pay for electricity provided by generator.

So here is a joke – a sick one – which has made the rounds:

The Collector is at the open door; he has a bill in his right hand and a pencil in his left. He holds out the bill to the woman standing on the threshold of her apartment. She must settle up for electricity supplied from a commercial generator, there having been less than six hours from the mains a day.

The woman thumbs through a number of 100,000 lira notes and hands them to the collector; she takes off a ring from her finger and her watch from her wrist and hands them over. Now she is bending down to take off her shoes ...

2021

Petrol Stationary

It is early October on a sunny Wednesday morning. My son-in-law, Nazih, glances at his dashboard and sees that he needs to fill up with petrol. He pulls off the *autostrade*, but there is no fuel to be had – not at IPT, Petronas, Medco or Total, nor at any outlet.

"What will you do?" I ask him.

He doesn't answer but gets on his phone. The conversation is short. He takes an exit off the *autostrade* and heads along the old coast road. A little way and we pull in at a deserted filling station. An attendant comes out of his cabin; there are brief exchanges. The attendant undoes the petrol cap and inserts the hose.

Back on the *autostrade,* I ask, "How did you manage that?"

"I know the distributor. He comes from Rahbeh, my village in the north."

"How will you repay him for the favour?"

"I have already done that; I punched him on the nose when we were at school together."

2021

The Camp

Nazih has taken me to a Palestinian refugee camp[1] at my request. It is situated along the coast from Beirut this side of Dog River. He approaches a middle-aged man smoking a cigarette, who recognises Nazih from his appearances on television. Nazih introduces me. The man stubs out the remains of his cigarette, shakes my hand, and we are invited into his house.... We sit round a table drinking Turkish coffee.

"My name is Imad," he says. "In 1948, my family fled from the fighting in Palestine. They were not allowed to return when Israel became a state."

"Were you born in Lebanon?" I ask.

"Yes, in this camp; my brother too. The camp started as a temporary refuge for Palestinians – for those of the Christian faith – but has grown into a permanent ramshackle network of thrown up buildings and narrow streets. We Palestinians in exile do not now expect to return to our homeland; our villages have been flattened and we are not welcome."

Nazih asks Imad if there are others, apart from Palestinians, living in the camp.

"There are some poor Lebanese families and a few Syrians who come to find work in this country and have stayed. It has become a large village and we know each other's problems and give help when needed. It is no longer a camp but a community."

"Are you able to make a living?" I ask.

"I am a plumber and get work when I can. A bank clerk now earns less than me because the Lebanese lira has lost most of its value. A clerk might earn the equivalent of a hundred US dollars a month, but I can do better with a plumbing job here and there."

"The camp is well situated," I remark.

Imad drains his coffee. "Yes, we have been fortunate. About ten years ago the Saudis built a luxury hotel, *Le Royal*, just down the slope from us in Dbayeh. I was fixing a leaking pipe there when the explosion at the port happened last summer. I didn't hear it, but my wife did; she said the crate of bottled water we keep on our roof garden jumped into the air. If you come up with me, I'll show you the view" – and we ascend a narrow flight of stairs …

"Look over there across the water to the port and the Beirut headland," Imad says. "Just below us" – and he points – "is the hotel I was talking about. Can you see the tops of the umbrella sun shades near the pool?"

We nod.

"The people who stay there may be rich, but looking out from my roof garden at the city beyond, I feel as though I am on top of the world."

Nazih and I stare across at the bay – and then, almost as an afterthought, Imad says, "But I can't forget my compatriots in other Arab camps who suffer because they cannot feel at home."

---

[1] *According to the United Nations Relief and Works Agency for Palestine Refugees in the Near East (UNRWA), in 2019 there were 475,075 Palestinian refugees registered in its twelve official refugee camps in Lebanon.*

2021

Dilemma of a Bank Clerk

Mohammed Hejazi has been employed by the Trust Bank for the last twelve years. He has worked in several local branches in the Southern Governorate gathering a variety of professional experience. Until a few years ago, Mohammed found it an occupation worth pursuing, because not only did he enjoy the work, but it also provided invaluable advantages: the Trust Bank insured his family against ill-health and even hospitalisation if needed – that is, for him, his wife and their three young children. The Bank also subsidised the children's education, which allowed Mohammed to send them to a private fee-paying school where the teaching was of a higher standard than it would have been at a government institution.

Although his salary had never been high, a certain amount of personal prestige was attached to the job. However, he had to supplement his pay by providing a weekend car-valet service at one of Saida's seaside restaurants; and at one time he opened a snack bar near the city centre which offered coffee, sandwiches and fruit juice, but had to give this up when the landlord demanded an unreasonable increase in rent for the premises. The old building was subsequently demolished and now a modern office block stands in its place.

This was Mohammed Hejazi's situation when in 2019 the value of the Lebanese lira collapsed on the open market from one thousand five hundred liras to the US dollar to a hundred thousand liras. This meant that his monthly salary was not nearly enough for his family to live on. Mohammed is only kept going by his brother, who emigrated to America ten years ago and who sends him regular remittances, enough to feed his family. Mohammed intends to repay his brother once Lebanon gets back on its financial feet. Unfortunately, there are few signs of recovery two years down the line.

Before the collapse of the currency, the Trust Bank had branches in every region: Akkar, Baalbek-Hermel, Beirut, Bekaa, Kesserwan-Jbeil, Mount Lebanon, Nabatieh and the North and South Governorates. There are now only three branches remaining – in Saida (where Mohammed is employed), Jbail and Tripoli – and these also are shortly to be closed, leaving only Trust Bank's central office in Beirut. But even if the Bank were to move Mohammed to a post there, he would find it impossible to make the daily journey from Saida; the cost of the fuel alone would consume his devalued salary.

Mohammed also worries that he may be fired. None of the banks in Lebanon are doing much business, due to the sustained currency restrictions imposed by the Central Bank, the virtual freezing of savings accounts and the devaluation of customer debt. Banks hardly have a function any more, apart from providing cash dispensers for the limited amount of funds permitted to be withdrawn each month. The banks' customers have resorted to money changing offices which have sprung up, like summer ants, all over the country – OMT, BOB, Whish, MoneyGram, Cash United, and Western Union – where they can change their dollars at high rates into wads of Lebanese liras. To crown it all, coronavirus has taken the lives of customers and accounts, and has put a further stop on business activity, particularly during pandemic lockdowns and when the international airport was closed.

So, what is Mohammed to do? Stay with the Trust Bank and carry on accepting charity from his brother in America? Or must he make the painful decision to leave his family in Saida, forfeit their free health insurance and children's subsidised education, and take a flight to Dubai to find whatever work is available there?

It is most likely he will depart because all trust in the banks in Lebanon has gone.

2021

On the Road to Tripoli

I am on the *autostrade* with Nazih at the wheel. He is a famous television actor; his comic roles have made everyone laugh from Sur in the south to Tripoli in the north. He has consoled them while Lebanon suffers economic pain. How they love him!

At this moment, he is holding his mobile phone in his right hand and the steering wheel in his left. He has been speaking at length. Perhaps there will be a film-shooting opportunity in these dire times.

I look in the side mirror and see a police car creeping up on us, become anxious and signal my son-in-law to cease his conversation and put down his phone. He takes no notice and carries on his conversation.

The police car has drawn level; we are now two vehicles abreast. I see the officer in the passenger seat looking across at us. Nazih waves at him with mobile in hand. The officer sticks out his arm – I think he will signal the driver to pull over – but no – with a wide smile the officer waves back. He has recognised the actor, Nazih Youssef, he who has lightened the lives of the Lebanese population. How they do love him!

2021

On a Tripoli Street

He sits in his car with the air conditioning on. The traffic is not moving. He lowers his window.

"What is happening up there?" he shouts to a teenage boy on a motorbike.

"A demonstration – at the electricity company."

The car creeps forward a metre or two. The driver sees multiple bunches of bananas hanging from a wooden frame by the roadside. He hoots his horn and shouts out, "Where is the banana man?"

A swarthy seller appears holding a cutlass-size knife. He cuts down a bunch and thrusts it through the driver's window. The driver thrusts several notes into the swarthy man's hand. The car moves forward a metre or two.

Before he has had time to close the car window, a woman in head-to-foot *shador*-black confronts the driver with cupped hands. The driver breaks off a banana from the bunch on the passenger seat and passes it out to the woman. The window slides shut and the car moves forward a metre or two.

On the central reservation there is a grubby-looking little girl, perhaps five or six years old, who has seen the driver passing something through his window. When she holds out her hands to him, the driver lowers his window, breaks off a banana from the bunch, holds it up in his left hand and in his right, a thousand lira note.

"Which one do you want?" he asks the little girl, who does not understand at first, never having had such choices. When she takes the worthless one thousand lira note, the driver places the banana in her free hand and closes the car window. The little girl looks on holding the note in one hand and the banana in the other.

The car is moving ahead – two – three – ten – twenty metres. The demonstration outside the electricity company must have dispersed; the traffic is moving forward fast. With his foot on the pedal, the driver glimpses a bent and bony old man sitting by the roadside. The car passes by leaving the bony man empty-handed.

2021

At a Beirut Pharmacy

The pharmacist was counting up the day's takings when a young man, wearing jeans and a soiled white T-shirt, came into the shop. Before the pharmacist had time to ask if he could help, the young man pulled out a pistol.

"If you want the money from the cash register, you can take all of it," the pharmacist said, trembling.

The young man simply shook his head.

"Do you want drugs?" the pharmacist asked, puzzled by his failure to speak.

The young man shook his head again.

"Then why are you pointing a gun at me? Say what you want and I will give it to you."

"Baby food," he replied hoarsely.

"I shall need to go into the back for that. How old is the baby?"

"She's four months."

The pharmacist was surprised that the young man did not follow him into the storeroom. "If I hadn't kept my phone in the shop, I could have contacted the police," he thought as he took down as many tins of the baby food as he could carry in the hope that his intruder would not demand the entire stock.

The young man lowered his pistol when he saw what the pharmacist had brought in.

"You see," he said, "my baby needs milk and I don't have enough liras. My wife can't feed her. Please forgive me," he said almost in tears – "and may Allah bless you," with which he swept the tins of baby food into a large plastic bag and left.

When the pharmacist picked up his mobile phone from under the counter to report what had happened, the phone had run out of charge.

2021

Safe

"How to keep one's money safe?" This question from a much-travelled businessman. I sip at my too-hot-coffee but can offer no reply.

"How, when the US dollar is draining out of Lebanon to war-exhausted Syria, and green notes fetch inflated rates in unofficial quarters?"

I shrug with despond. "I've no idea. To safe havens outside the country, I suppose."

"But that's not possible. It's only corrupt politicians who can do that – millions, perhaps billions, exported by those in the know who should know better." He gesticulates in despair. "All this while the Lebanese lira loses its value by the day and the locals become even poorer than they were before the plunge."

"To be sure, there's no safety in their earnings while prices rise so rapidly."

The much-travelled businessman takes a bite out of his hundred-thousand-lira croissant. "Even those with legitimate savings are faced with certain dilemma. Where can one keep one's money? There's no safekeeping at a bank if you can't take out the sums needed."

"And what is business to do while withdrawals are restricted?" I ask. "Commerce won't continue without ready cash."

"The traffic of trade will be jammed; shopkeepers will pull down their shutters and suppliers shut up their unsold wares. That's what will happen – has happened already. Lebanon won't be a trading nation anymore."

Sitting at a table next to ours is a woman wearing heavy horn-rimmed glasses and large round earrings. She speaks: "You say you don't know where to keep your money. I can help you with that."

"Oh, please do," responds the much-travelled businessman.

"It can be bought in several sizes and screwed firmly to the wall. There is a secret code known only to the owner. Twist the dial and the door opens to your private store of cash. Safety can be found in a safe. You can bank on it. Can I interest you in buying one?"

2022

At a Bank in Beirut

Let's call him Sadik, a man of moral integrity, for he has cultivated the land and has traded honestly. He has built up a business and considerable capital – 200,000 US dollars to be precise – deposited at a Beirut Bank. But one could hardly call it an investment in these times of economic collapse, for the bank is offering no interest and Sadik cannot withdraw his money in large quantities because the authorities at the Central Bank have decreed it. He would have been willing to wait for the country's financial recovery, but now his father urgently needs expensive medical attention – a heart transplant no less. Without such treatment, he will die in a matter of months. Sadik must have access to his dollars (so, too, his brother who has money at the same bank) before his father can have his operation.

This is where the story begins. In good faith, Sadik called in at his bank in Beirut[1] and asked to withdraw his entire savings – in cash. The bank clerk could not oblige. Sadik went home, forlorn and frustrated, picked up his telephone and arranged for an appointment with the Manager of the bank. But when the meeting took place a few days later, the Manager was adamant that no such large sum could be withdrawn, in spite of his client's constant pleading.

Sadik's despair turned to fierce anger. He visited the bank again and protested, demanding his money in a loud voice. He refused to leave and was escorted out of the building by two hefty security men.

By now, his anger had become ferocious and he was more determined than ever to recover his 200,000 dollars, if not by fair means – by foul.

We see him now approaching the bank holding a large metal can in his right hand and his mobile phone in his left. It so happens that the security men are taking a furtive break for coffee and a smoke at a nearby café; this allows Sadik to enter without being noticed.

Once inside, he takes in his surroundings. A woman with streaky blonde hair sits at the reception desk with a small coffee cup at her elbow; three consultation cubicles are occupied, another empty; several seated clients wait for their turn to be served. He notes that the door to the Manager's office is closed. Sadik takes a number from the dispenser, sits down and places the metal can on the vacant seat next to him. The digital clock on the wall reads 11.35. It is 12.05 when his number is called. Sadik puts his mobile phone in his hip pocket and takes hold of the metal can. Standing in front of the counter he recognises the bank clerk who has served him before. From behind his glass panel, the clerk recognises Sadik– an awkward customer who will not take no for an answer.

"For the last and final time, I demand to have my money – all of it!" and Sadik holds up the metal can.

"No, Sir, I cannot," replies the clerk. "And please do not threaten me."

"If you don't listen, I shall burn this bank down, do you hear me?"

(The clerk presses an alert button under the counter.) "No, Sir, it will be of no use."

But Sadik, undeterred, unscrews the lid of the metal can and begins pouring the contents onto the floor of the bank and through the hole in the counter's glass panel. The clerk falls over backwards in his chair. The liquid gives off a strong smell of gasoline.

By this time, the clients are standing up in horror – is this man crazy or is he holding up the bank? Sadik turns to face them, but before he can say anything, he sees the Manager at his office door with a rifle in his hands.

"Leave here immediately," shouts the Manager.

"Give me that gun or I shall set your bank alight" – and Sadik takes out a lighter from his trouser pocket and flicks on the flame. The clients gasp in unison.

"Please be sensible," the Manager pleads.

"Then give me the gun. Drop it on the floor in the middle of the room."

With the intruder clicking his lighter on and off, the Manager has no choice but to obey.

"You won't get your money this way," says the Manager.

Sadik picks up the rifle and fixes his eyes on the Manager and looks at him as though he were an insect. "Do you want to see this bank burnt to the ground?" – but the Manager gives no reply.

"Let him have his money," says a man holding a bulky plastic bag and wearing a shabby baseball cap. "For that matter, give me *my* money." – and looking around – "Give us all our money!"

Sadik observes some of the clients nodding in agreement. He hears a woman whimpering.

"Please let us go," she moans. "My husband will be worried about me."

At this point, the automatic door of the bank entrance slides open and the two security men enter; their faces drop in horrified disbelief.

"Come in!" commands Sadik pointing the rifle at them. "Stand over there – by the water fountain."

Sadiq turns to the whimpering woman. "Leave!" he says to her, and gesticulating to the clients – "You others, go too!"

They move hurriedly to the open door. The Manager makes to move with them.

"You are staying here," Sadik says, "and your staff – all of them – and you two!" pointing to the security men.

The sound of police sirens can now be heard in the distance.

"Give yourself up before more harm is done," says the Manager sounding a little more confident.

Sadik ignores him and pulls shut the security gate at the entrance to the bank. "Sit down all of you!" He points to a row of seats with the rifle. "You shall stay here until I get my money," and adds with a touch of irony: "Make yourselves comfortable."

*   *   *

For several hours, a police officer has been talking to the "terrorist". He has exchanged mobile numbers with him but has failed to persuade him to call off his hold-up. It appears to the police officer that this is a simple case of attempted robbery, perhaps to fund terrorist activities. It is fortunate that he and his colleagues have arrived at the bank in time before the criminal can make his escape. His main concern now is to free the remaining hostages held inside the bank.

*   *   *

Sadik is waiting to hear from the police officer. He realises that the police officer does not believe the motive for his actions.

"You can't expect him to accept the reason you have given," the Manager says. "It is too absurd."

Sadik is angered by these remarks. "It is not absurd to want to withdraw my money left in the bank's safekeeping if it is not kept safe for me to take out."

"The bank no longer has the dollars you want. You are wasting your time."

"And why does the bank have no dollars? I'll tell you why; because before the crash of the lira your interest rates were too high. You thought you could tempt people to invest in your bank and failed. You miscalculated."

"At least you had the benefit of the high interest rates – everything was rosy for a number of years. Why should you complain?"

"I invested in your bank in good faith. You are the monetary expert. Why should I pay for your mistakes?" – but before the Manager can reply, Sadik's mobile rings. "You take it," he says to the Manager handing him the phone. "Perhaps they will listen to you. You had better persuade them if you want to leave this bank alive."

*   *   *

It is now evening and the Manager, who is keen to go home to his wife and children after prolonged and exhausting negotiation, has brokered a deal with the Internal Security Forces (ISF) at the Interior Ministry. Sadik will be allowed to withdraw 35,000 US dollars in order to cover the expense of his father's operation. It has also been agreed with the police that he will not be prosecuted for holding up the bank.

*   *   *

I am in the middle of a huge crowd of spectators assembled outside the bank. LBC and MTV are conducting interviews with the wife and brother of the hostage-taker. On my mobile phone I hear his brother saying, "Everybody should do the same as Sadik to get their money out."

I hear someone in the crowd shout, "Down with the rule of the banks!" Claps of approval. Media cameras flash. The blue lights of police cars blink on and off. An ambulance, arriving, whines to a halt. The word has got round that a deal with the hostage-taker has been agreed. The atmosphere in the crowd turns to one of jolly carnival. Some start to sing. The iron gate of the bank is opened from the inside and the hostages come out. The spectators quieten as the hostages are escorted into a police van and are driven away with siren sounding.

All eyes are turned again to the entrance of the bank. I can hear weapons being cocked by crouching marksmen. The crowd, held back by a cordon of policemen, falls silent. The hostage-taker appears. A police officer shouts, "Put your hands on your head!" The hostage-taker raises his right hand; two fingers form into a victory sign. The voice of a woman in the crowd cries out, "You are our hero!" A few in the crowd begin to clap. Another voice imitates the call, "You are our hero!" Others join in, "You are our hero!" The chorus gathers volume until we are all singing in unison, "You are our hero! You are our hero! You are our hero!"

---

[1] *The name of the protagonist and many of the details concerning what happened in Beirut on 11th August, 2022, have been fictionalised. "Facts" reported in the media did not always agree; nor was it the first time an incident of its kind had occurred during Lebanon's financial crisis. Other similar incidents were to follow. Only when the banks closed their doors to the public, did the hold-ups stop.*

2023

On the Hour – More or Less

It is the last Sunday in March and the Holy Month of Ramadan has just begun. On Saturday night, clocks will leap forward to summer time. *Iftar* – the breaking of the fast – will come an hour later. Long-sitting Speaker of the House, who will himself refrain from food and drink from sunrise to sunset, thinks this punitive. He has asked the Prime Minister to stop the clocks so that *Iftar* is earlier for Moslems. To his satisfaction, the Prime Minister, who will likewise abstain, agrees. He sends out a decree and at midnight the clocks and watches of Lebanon mark time for an hour while those in temperate lands advance.

When the sun rises from behind Lebanon's mountain peaks, confusion ensues: itineraries are put out of joint, flight times put back at short notice, business meetings cancelled or postponed, engagements re-scheduled, work rotas revised, and computer time adjusted. Temporal turbulence leads to complaint from all quarters, except perhaps by some who see advantage in an hour gained. The Speaker of the House is mocked, the Prime Minister rattled.

Regretting the Speaker's persuasive words, the Prime Minister orders a timely reversal: catch-up, fast forward – synchronicity regained. Flight times are advanced, meetings again rearranged, original work rotas restored and computer time re-reset.

But to those who fast in the Holy Month of Ramadan it makes no difference whether an hour – more or less – will put *Iftar* forward or back; they'll not be living by a clock made by man, but will break fast when the red globe of the sun has sunk into the sea and the muezzin has let out his call to evening prayer.

2023

A Commemoration

Politicians and dignitaries have come together to remember soldiers of the Lebanese Armed Forces kidnapped and beheaded by Syrian militant groups, Daesh and Al-Nousra, at Arsal, a town in the Bekaa Valley. The soldiers are hailed as martyrs.

The ceremony takes place at Ballouneh, eighteen kilometres north of the capital at a height of 650 metres, in an ecological garden under a hot summer sun. Officials of the Organisation for Tradition and Nature are present, accompanied by members of the municipality dressed in best suits. A much-decorated general joins them in the front row, placing his cap on his lap. Opposite sit representatives of the country's religious communities: Druze imam wearing cylindrical white headdress; Sunni's bowl-like white hat with red lid; and Shia's pale turban – all black-robed, as are hatless Orthodox and Maronite priests. Behind them, citizens from the country's four corners, women widowed at Arsal, men whose friends died there, fatherless children and those who come to pay their respects to the fallen. They sit in a U shape with a large Lebanese cedar-tree flag – symbol of eternity, steadiness, happiness and prosperity – draped before them. The sun beats down. Guests sweat; the heads of the hatless glisten with perspiration.

The ceremony begins: an army anthem is sung, the singer adorned in sable frock. Spectators stand and sing with her; the general is rigid in salute; all applaud at anthem's end. Speeches follow, some remembered verbatim, others from white paper. A poem is spoken with passion. After more speeches, the children are called to be handed gifts wrapped in silver paper. The adults disperse for refreshment.

This gathering together of Lebanon's united denizens happened in a nurtured garden. The day following, the country's Prime Minister called his cabinet to the palace at Baabda to discuss the appointment of a new President. They could meet with no agreement[1].

---

[1] *A president was not agreed upon until January 2025*

2023/2024

War Returns

Near Kibbutz Re'im, Southern Israel

They have called the festival the Supernova Sukkot Gathering. It is a holiday celebration. The music lovers and dancers have stopped to see the sun rise. They are high on ecstasy and the blue Earth is a wonderful place. When the empty sky is alight, it is suddenly filled with streaks of smoke coming from the nearby Gaza strip. At first, the stupefied festival goers are dazed by it. They do not know that those in the ghetto have broken out, the Al-Aqsa Flood released. The fighters are high on hatred and armed with rocket-propelled grenades, mines, sniper rifles and drones. They are out to kill and capture those they call "filthy dogs". The festival goers will hide in bushes and orchards, in roadside skips, garbage bins and bomb shelters; they will run, they will be shot, they will be taken as hostages, driven away, some alive, some already dead.

It is the day when Gaza has broken out. Bulldozers have torn down the abhorred frontier fences; pickup trucks loaded with fighters accelerate into their stolen land; more follow on motorbikes. From the sea, speedboats hurtle towards the outlawed shore; powered paragliders descend set on destruction. At Sderot, one kilometre from the border, the police station is overrun, personnel – men and women – executed, computer systems smashed. The military base at Re'im is captured, its soldiers killed; watchtowers attacked from above by drones; a pylon destroyed. At Nahal Oz, fifty men and women summarily dispatched. Kibbutzniks are slaughtered at Nirim, Nir Oz, Nir Yitzhak, Netiv HaAsara, and Kfar Aza. And those who reside in Be'eri, their doors broken open and killed or captured. This day will be remembered by the new nation as the Simchat Torah Massacre.

Gaza, 7th October 2024

Towns are pounded to rubble in year-long relentless retaliation, its population decimated in armed pursuit of Hamas men, and hostages, hidden in the tunnels of the "Gaza Metro". Hospitals and schools are hit, patients turned to ashes; tower blocks crumble into concrete, residents buried. The dead are many thousands – women and children, old and young, healthy and sick – the wounded tens of thousands, the traumatised uncountable. Women weep countless tears; they cannot be consoled. Children roam in the rubble of their homes. Young men are rounded up, stripped and driven off for interrogation. Displaced families carry all they have south where many take refuge in makeshift tents on beaches or on open land. Hunger haunts the population, disease creeps in. A second wretched winter awaits them.

All the while to the north across the border in Lebanon, Hezbollah fighters respond to the carnage in Gaza with rocket firepower aimed at Galilee and beyond. They will not cease until the Gaza strip is relieved of deadly drones, artillery fire, missiles and shelling, the destruction of homes, and the slaughter of its people. But such impudence Zion will not tolerate. Beirut will be battered in-tit-for-tat reprisal; so too Sur on the coast, Baalbek in the Bekaa valley, and Nabatieh south of the Litani river – little Lebanon once more suffering the returns of war – destruction, displacement and distress.

* * *

It is time to leave a country overtaken by rancour. I sit with my family in a restaurant above the Jeita caves, prepared to take flight to England. The road below is filled with traffic on its way up to the safety of mountain villages. The sky is October blue. Then I see them overhead, cranes, wings moving in unison – a flock migrating in tight V formation. I marvel at their long journey from Scandinavia to lands south of Lebanon – to North Africa, Ethiopia, or nearer home, to the Houleh Valley in Galilee. Later, I read of Africans in the Sahel who hold cranes to be sacred – their arrival brings peace. Would that these birds bore a lasting harmony to the Levant

Part Four: Last Lines

2125

Lebanon: An Unlikely Utopia

My name is Tom More Johae and I have come by sailing vessel to this country at the eastern end of the Mediterranean in the role of ambassador from King William VII of England. I shall reside with my friend, Abdulatif Nazrallah from the port of Sur, who will take me along the coast by train, and up the mountains and down into the valley, in the next few days. He will show me what has been accomplished since the cataclysms of the twenty-first century, those which overcame the countries of the region, but which led to the end of suspicion and hostilities prevailing between them.

Having arrived in high summer, I can see, from the train, the red roofs of coastal buildings, those built in the early style after the macroseisms and tsunami of the last century. Abdulatif points to the twin chimneys of what was once an oil-powered station at Zouk Mosbeh.

"Surprisingly, they survived the tremors and the tsunami which followed," he says.

"Why were the chimneys not knocked down if they had no more use?"

"The philosophers decided to keep it as a token – a memorial – to the lack of vision of past rulers. Apparently, the chimneys emitted smoke without stop – that is, until the oil supply ran out. You can imagine how polluted the air in the mountains and along the coast became, and how it must have affected the health of those living under such murky skies. Petrol-driven cars added to the problem, and private oil generators too, because of the unreliable supply of mains electricity in those days."

"You mention cars as a cause of air pollution. Why have you not opted for electric-powered vehicles?"

Abdulatif nods vigorously. "A good question. The problem – an ecological one – lies with the raw materials required in the manufacture of a car battery, such as lithium, manganese and cobalt, which have to be mined and the resources are not without limit. Furthermore, when the life of the battery is over, not only are the contents not recyclable, but there is also a problem of waste disposal. This is why our vehicles are powered by hydrogen."

"Which means the only byproduct when used in a fuel cell is water."

"Precisely."

I sit back in my seat on the train and stare out of the window.

"I've observed that there are very few wind farms. How do you account for this since you told me that only recyclable energy is used to supply the population?"

"Lebanon rarely experiences strong winds, which is why wind farms are few; but we do have plenty of harnessed water from the country's many mountain streams and rivers. Reservoirs provide ample drinking water, some of which is piped to neighbouring countries where water is short. Hydro-electricity is also another source of energy which can be exported. The construction of dams for these purposes did cause some concerns for ecological reasons, but we have tried to compensate by reintroducing flora and fauna to other mountain areas which had been stripped of natural life in previous centuries."

I put it to Abdulatif that he has said nothing about the sun as a source of energy.

"Well, you will have seen the roofs on the buildings of the littoral. There is not a single home in this country without solar powered pantile roofs. Our mountainous terrain makes it possible for all our villages to have exposure to the sun, even when in the winter the sun is low."

Abdulatif gets up from his seat. "Now let's go to the buffet car and drink a cup of coffee."

We have been making our way along the coast by electric train. The local two-track line stretches from Sur in the south to Debnine in the north. I have observed passengers getting on and off at the numerous stops. Abdulatif tells me that all public transport in twenty-second-century Lebanon is free.

"This is why you see so few cars," he explains. "Once Lebanon seemed to have been colonised by cars, there were so many. But the railway line helped to alter the dominance of motor vehicles. However, shuttles are plentiful. When you get off the train, an auto-shuttle will take you the rest of the way to your destination if it is local."

"What if your village is in the mountains?"

"You take the cable car."

I am puzzled by this answer.

"Haven't you noticed them as we have been travelling along the coast? The idea came from the original one at Jounieh; it used to take tourists up to the cathedral. Then, after the wars in the last century, a much longer cable car route was constructed reaching up to Mount Sannine."

"Why there in particular?"

"Because it gave the opportunity to develop a ski resort which, as you will know, is now one of the most sought after on the globe."

"Why so popular?"

"You see, Lebanon lies well to the south compared with other world ski resorts, and benefits from plenty of winter sunshine. Not only that, in the summer when it is hot on the coast, you can take a cable car up to the Mount, where it is cooler, and stay at a hotel, or in one of the chalets."

As Abdulatif is speaking, I become aware the train is slowing down.

"We are coming to a cable-car station," he says, opening the electric-controlled window. "These stations line the coast so that you can take a cable car up to your village. Those who have vehicles of their own are not permitted to drive down to towns at sea level but must take a cable car. It will terminate at a cable-car station on the coast, and the traveller can then get on a train going north or south depending on the intended destination. If you want to travel beyond Lebanon, you can change at Sur for a train on the railway line to Cairo, or at Debnine to continue through Syria en route for Istanbul."

"I don't want to leave Lebanon just yet," I say with a smile.

"We don't want you to leave, Tom. There is a lot more I want to show you."

*   *   *

Today we are in the Bekaa Valley. Abdulatif, whose family originally came from Baalbek, a garden city in the north, is keen to tell me about the area.

"Farm produce has always been plentiful here," he says. "If you want to know more about what has been grown in the past, I suggest you read an evocative description written by your forbear, Antony Johae.[1] However, farming methods in the twenty-first century were not always the most efficient or ecologically wise. The soil gradually eroded through overuse and it wasn't until the philosophers introduced land reforms reverting to ancient dryland practice that the soil regained its fertility."

"Could you explain what that entails?"

"Simply, the land is ploughed and tilled, but left fallow every other seeding season. This allows the soil to gain moisture and to be revitalised. The yield in the following year then becomes higher. There is no need to supplement with toxic chemical fertilisers."

I look across the expanse of the flat land, at a glitter of greenhouses, at patches of black soil, stretches of wheat, golden in the sunshine, maize standing tall, long rows of green vine, some diagonal on slight slopes, others vertical and horizontal; sprawling orchards, winding streams and little irrigation lakes; and straight and curling roads, lined with cypress trees which throw their sharp shadows onto the tarmac.

"Come!" my guide commands. "Let us to the city of Zahle so that you can taste the local wine."

*   *   *

Abdulatif has taken me on a cable car high up to mountains in the north of the country. As we hang over the high terrain, I can see steep slopes covered thick with trees.

"You see the cedars, Tom. They have been our lifeline. Before large-scale replanting, the cutting down of the cedars over the centuries was partly the reason for temperatures warming and causing a lack of snow in winter. This, in turn, led to a shortage of water in the long summer months."

"A sort of downward spiral."

"Exactly. The depletion of the forests had been going on for centuries. As long ago as four thousand years, the cedar forests were mentioned in the epic, *Gilgamesh.*" Abdulatif gets out a book from his rucksack. "In this history, you can read of the cedar." He turns the pages. "Yes, here we are. *'On the mountain the cedars uplift their abundance. Their shadow is beautiful, is all delight. Thistles hide under them, and the dark prick-thorn; sweet-smelling flowers hide under the cedars ... in all directions, ten thousand miles stretches that forest.'"*

"Thank you, Abdullatif. But isn't that a bit of an exaggeration – 'ten thousand miles'?"

"Hyperbole, certainly, but it leaves one in no doubt about the extensiveness of the cedar forests and the wonder felt by their vastness. The trees were said to be protected by the Mesopotamian gods and were seen as divine because no other tree can grow at such a high altitude as the cedar. However, this did not prevent Gilgamesh building the city of Uruk out of cedars."

"That would have meant cutting down a lot of trees!"

"And that was only the start. The resin and sawdust of the cedar was used by the ancient Egyptians in the process of embalming their rulers. They also built boats with cedar wood, as did the Phoenicians, the early inhabitants of this land. The Assyrians, Babylonians, Greeks, Romans, and Persians all constructed houses and temples from the cedar."

"And King Soloman for the Temple in Jerusalem."

"Yes, for him as for many, the cedar was 'the first of trees.' The Hebrews also applied the peel of the Lebanese cedar in circumcision and for the treatment of leprosy."

"But you wouldn't need to cut down many trees for medicinal purposes, would you?" I interject.

"No, but later, in the nineteenth century when the Levant was under the Ottomans, the destruction of the cedar forests was extensive. Cedar wood provided the fuel for railway engines because it burned better than other woods. And in the twentieth century during the Second World War, British troops destroyed most of what was left of the forests in the process of laying track for railways lines. Unfortunately, they were not lines laid for Lebanon."

"I am sorry my people were responsible for degrading your landscape."

"No matter, Tom. The days of the indiscriminate exploitation of nature are over. Now all nations live in harmony with the natural world, and with one another, as you and I on our journey to the cedar heights of Lebanon."

As Abdulatif and I descend in the cable car to the littoral below, I am reminded of a saying of the ancient Arabian Prophet: *"There will come a time when the whole world will be illuminated and there will be no more darkness. On that day, Lebanon will be the most illuminated of all places."*

---

[1] *The reference is to "Bekaa's Bounty" which appears on page 25*

Antony Johae - Biography

Antony Johae (b. 1937, Chiswick, UK), gained his Ph.D. from the University of Essex in 1979: a comparative study of dream and symbolism in Dostoevsky and Kafka. He went on to teach literature in Ghana, Tunisia and Kuwait before retiring to Lebanon (his wife's country of origin) and to Colchester in Essex. He has published five poetry collections: *Poems of the East* (Gipping Press, 2015); *After-Images: Homage to Éric Rohmer* (Poetry Salzburg, 2019); *Ex-Changes* (The High Window, 2020); *Home Poems* (Orphean Press, 2022); and *Foreign Forays: Poems of Travel in Europe and the Med* (Mica Press, 2025).

Palewell Press

Palewell Press is an independent publisher handling poetry, fiction and non-fiction with a focus on books that foster Justice, Equality and Sustainability.

The Editor can be reached on enquiries@palewellpress.co.uk

www.ingramcontent.com/pod-product-compliance
Lightning Source LLC
Chambersburg PA
CBHW052104070526
44584CB00017B/2323